YES

NO

MAYBE

On my experiences with sex, sexual assault,

And sexual education.

Dedicated with love to my Mom and Papa who taught

me the meaning of strength,

to Emily for being proof of true friendship,

And to each and every survivor of sexual assault.

...Introduction...

Human nature is a complex ever-changing maze. There is no handbook. There is no universal set of rules. You have to learn how to adapt to different people, jobs, and situations. Your parents or guardians try to teach you how to maneuver through the world but they have only their own experiences to guide them. And there is no way to be prepared. Every single situation is dependent on the other people involved.

I am not very old. Some of you will say that I haven't lived enough life to have any real opinion. But I have twenty-three years of experience. I have had bad days and good days. I have been helped, hurt, heard, and ignored. I have been healthy, sick, happy, and depressed. Had friends, lost friends, fell in love, and fallen out of love. So even though I am only twenty-three, I have lived. I have traveled and been exposed to a few different cultures and have read about even more. My parents exposed me to as much as possible because they wanted me to see how expansive and incredible the world around me is. They wanted me to exercise my mind as I grew up, so they gave me piano lessons, then violin lessons, and at one point, even guitar lessons. I don't remember how to play any of those, but I am glad I had the chance to find out if they were my passion. My grandparents and extended family are Catholic so my parents sent me to one of those religious after-school programs. My mom also taught me about Buddhism, Taoism, Judaism, and introduced me to other religions and spiritual beliefs. Then she told me I could believe whatever I wanted. I consider myself a spiritual person, but I don't abide by any one faith. So in reality, my mom and dad did the best they could to prepare me for the future. They punished me when I misbehaved and congratulated me when I did well. They made sure I knew how to be respectful to the people around me and tried to help me learn the difference between respect and letting people take advantage of me. I am not great at standing up for myself, but I keep learning. I keep trying. But there are a lot of things in this world that parents can't prepare you for.

This is the story of a moment that nothing could have prepared me for. This is the true story of a moment that not one ounce of education or experience could prepare me for. This is the story of

my sexual assault.

…Define Sexual Assault and Rape…

"You were in a relationship. You had sex with him the night before and you let him sleep over in bed with you. So stop overreacting. He didn't sexually assault you. He was just horny and did not want to wake you up."

Those were the first words I read when I asked for advice anonymously on a part of reddit.com about sex. The anonymous author continued on to tell me that he had touched and slept with his girlfriend multiple times when she had been asleep or passed out from alcohol. I decided, after reading this, to call a therapy hotline.

The therapist I called told me that I had not been very smart to have sex with a man I met on Tinder two months ago. How could I know anything about him in such a short amount of time? Obviously, I should have realized something bad could happen. Obviously, it was my fault for letting him into my life and my apartment.

The therapist I met with weekly for my anxiety, depression, and PTSD told me it was probably just a misunderstanding. We should invite him to a session so I could hear his side of the story. I shouldn't overreact and label this incident as something before he had a chance to explain.

So I texted him, "I just need to know, if I hadn't pushed you away would you have had sex with me? I just really need you to tell me the truth. And please be honest. I won't press charges. I just need to have you admit it to me. Please I need to know for my own healing. I just need you to admit it. I won't press charges but please tell me if you were going to continue if I hadn't woken up."

"Yeah."

According to the Rape, Abuse, and Incest National Network (RAINN), the nations anti-sexual assault organization, sexual assault is "sexual contact or behavior that occurs without explicit consent of the victim." Some forms of sexual assault include:

Penetration of the victim's body, also known as rape.

Attempted rape.

Forcing a victim to perform sexual acts, such as oral sex or penetrating the perpetrator's body.

Fondling or unwanted sexual touching.

Rape, according to the FBI website, is defined as "penetration, no matter how slight, of the vagina or anus with any body part or object, or oral penetration by a sex organ of another person without consent of the victim." But when you're assaulted, every state and every person has a different view on whether or not what happened to you was rape, sexual assault, or just you overreacting to a situation.

There is not one day that goes by without me asking myself whether I was sexually assaulted or raped. I research the different definitions plastered all over the internet once a week to try to figure it out. I even try to just close my eyes and ask myself which label feels like it fits sometimes because I feel like I am going crazy. So generally, I just call it a sexual assault. His penis never entered me, so it cannot be rape right? Now months later I know that it does have a specific name; digital rape.

I am a victim and a survivor of an attack that I cannot even name without offending someone; without being lectured by someone as to how I am wrong about what happened to me. It has been almost four months since that morning, and I still feel like I am fighting the world. When I want to tell someone what happened to me, what do I say? What do I call it? What did I survive? This is my reality.

I am trying to pass my first year of law school. Trying to have a normal adult sex life, normal relationships, normal social interactions. I am trying to live with the anxiety, depression, and

PTSD I have had for years but only just started getting help for this summer. Because, this summer, I finally admitted to my family that I had no control over my breakdowns. That the few times I had scratched my wrist till it bled were obviously a sign that something was wrong. And on top of all of this, now, I have to live with a constant confusion of an attack that is slowly driving me insane. This is my reality.

...I Froze When He Touched Me...

"He did what any respectable guy who wakes up next to the woman he spent the night before railing would think to do: continue the night into the morning."

"Dude was probably still turned on by your sex earlier in the night. Saying you were assaulted seems like an overstatement."

"That isn't assault or rape... Unless you specifically told him you don't want him to do that."

"You sleep together in the same bed, are you telling me he isn't allowed to touch you?"

These are just a few of the anonymous responses I got when I posted what happened to me anonymously to try and get advice. This is the true story of that morning:

11

I woke up and just froze. I was lying on my right side with my back to him. I cannot remember if I was wearing pajama pants or not, but I am fairly certain I was not. We had had sex the night before. I knew it was morning because of the light coming through the window. But it wasn't the light that had woken me up. It was the fact that his hand was in between my legs, his fingers inside my body, inside my vagina. But he wasn't trying to get my attention in any other way. He was not kissing my neck or whispering my name. Was not nudging me awake or anything remotely like that. His fingers were just playing inside me. We had spoken about trying new things, but not once had we discussed morning sex or sex while one of us was sleeping. If we had I would have told him absolutely not. I want to be awake for sex no matter what. If you want sex, wake me up. I would have told him that, had he told me that sex while I was asleep, was something he was into. But I never got that chance.

I couldn't move from the shock. Why was he not trying to wake me up if he was horny? Did he care that I was not awake when he started? I made no move to alert him to the fact that I was awake. Because I was scared of the possibilities. Scared of how he would act if I reacted to this new type of touch. I was scared that if I tried to move away he would become forceful. He was completely silent behind me. His breathing proof of the fact that he was fully awake. Then he started shifting. I could tell that he was pulling off his boxers. And we both remained silent as he positioned himself for penetration. I fully realized what was about to happen, and finally found a small amount of courage. I used one hand to push him away. But I still said nothing. I did not turn to look at him. I just pushed. Before I could breathe out and relax, his hand came back. It was about to be inside me again.

"No. I don't want to." I was able to say no. I pushed him away again, still refusing to look at him.

"Yes. You're ready. I know you are. I made you ready." His hand was back. I pushed him away one last time and this time it stopped. A few minutes later without any words, he fell back asleep. I waited until I was sure his breathing was even enough to tell me he was back in a deep sleep and I finally managed to move.

I sat up hugging my knees to my chest. I could not even look at him. The man who had brought me flowers and chocolate just three weeks before — I could not recognize him. I kept replaying the last, fifteen minutes in my head. I was shaking, trying to figure out if I should confront him, if it was safe to bring it up. I got out of the bed and at that point I do know I had put pajamas on. I still can't remember when exactly I had put them on. I was pacing. Back and forth. Back and forth. My taser was in the bureau near my window. Should I get it out? I stood for a while away from the bed. My dance pole was set up in that corner away from the bed. I stood next it and leaned on it for a while. I had started pole dancing last February. It had given me so much confidence in both my body and in my social abilities. It was my rock. So I leaned on it as I started to cry. I called out his name twice to wake him up. Standing against my pole.

"You tried to have sex with me while I was asleep. I said no and you said yes, that you knew I was ready."

He sat up, still half asleep. At first he denied it, then he told me it was true and he was sorry. He moved to the foot of the bed and for some reason I came back to the bed sitting as far from him as possible. Hugging my knees to my chest. Shaking. Crying. He told me again he was sorry. That he would do whatever I needed to help me trust him again. He asked me what I needed. I told him to leave. I wanted to call a hotline, watch some TV, and calm down. He agreed, but said he wouldn't leave me in this state. After all, he was to blame. I told him again that I wanted to be alone. I wanted to call my therapy hotline, watch TV, and calm down. He asked me not to press charges. He wasn't going to leave me when he was the reason for my frazzled state. I was scared. I told him I was scared and to leave. Again he asked me not to press charges. He would do whatever I wanted but he didn't want to leave me like this.

It took an hour to convince him. A whole hour. I called a therapy hotline needing advice and comfort.

"You only knew him two months and you let him stay over? You can't know someone after only two months. At least now you know to be a little bit

smarter next time you meet someone on Tinder or

OkCupid."

It was an older female on the other line. Her words crushed me. I felt stupid. Pathetic. Angry. Confused. So so confused. I only knew my last boyfriend for a month before he told me he loved me. We had stayed together for seven months. We loved each other very much. I had never dated someone for more than a month before sleeping with them and had never had this type of experience before. I hung up on her, made myself some food, and sat in bed with Netflix. I wrote down what had happened. I posted it to the subreddit for sex questions on reddit.com. I needed advice, needed clarity.

"He did what any respectable guy who wakes up next to the woman he spent the night before railing would think to do: continue the night into the morning."

"Dude was probably still turned on by your sex earlier in the night. Saying you were assaulted seems like an overstatement."

"That isn't assault or rape... Unless you specifically told him you don't want him to do that."

"You sleep together in the same bed, are you telling me he isn't allowed to touch you?"

Those responses were echoing in my mind as I got ready for the Halloween party at the bar. I had picked out my outfit months ago. It would be my first Halloween party at my law school. It was at the town bar that had reopened just a few weeks ago. I had a black steampunk corset, fishnet stockings, ruffle booty shorts, latex knee high boots, a mini pirate hat, and goggles. The outfit had made me feel incredibly sexy, badass, and powerful when I had tried it on the week before. Now it felt a bit off. But I had been looking forward to this party for weeks. I could not miss it. I walked across the town square and felt a bit jumpy, a bit on edge. But I tried to ignore that. I got to the dance and it was so loud. I got a free beer and hit the dance floor.

Have you ever had an out of body moment? Where you felt like a passenger in your own body who has no control? I felt so disconnected from the world around me during that party. I did not want anything to do with the happy people. So after just forty minutes I left. Walked back across the town square, up my apartment stairs, changed back into pajamas, and called the therapy hotline again.

This time the woman on the other line was supportive. There was no judgement, no blame, just comfort. I started cooking some more food as we spoke. I got off the phone, brought the food to my room, took three Klonopin pills, and watched tv until I fell asleep.

Before I continue telling you about what happened after that morning, I want to tell you about my sexual past. I need you to understand or at least know the background I had in matters of sex and relationships.

...Sex and I Before...

I got my first period around age eleven. My school gave me sex ed. They put me with other girls and we watched a movie with our moms about how are body develops. It explained that my body would be changing, how the basics of sex work, the dangers of pregnancy and STDs, and informed us what condoms and birth control were. My mom told me about masturbation and helped me understand that if I got feelings "down there" that was normal healthy and I could pleasure myself if I wanted to. She even told me that sex was normal and healthy if you were smart about it. That I shouldn't be in a hurry to be with a guy but that when I was ready and with someone I trusted to respect me it was ok to have sex. That I could come to her with any problems.

I had my first kiss at seventeen. I was in college around a lot of attractive men and I finally told my mom that I wanted birth control. She had asked if I wanted it before I left for school but I had said no. She had told me at some point after that it was ok and normal to kiss someone you are not in love with. Love is great, but it isn't neccessary. In December during a game of strip poker when I admitted to not having had a kiss, a friend leaned over and kissed me. I was naked. He had on only boxers. It was amazing and freeing and I have never forgotten it. I wasn't in love. We weren't alone. But it was an awesome first kiss and I have never for one moment regretted it.

I fooled around later that year with a man ten years older than me. We had met while blues dancing and flirted heavily. He invited me to a movie at my school and afterwards, as we were headed to the same dance, he offered to drive me. We had to stop at his office so he could drop something off. During the tour, we rounded a corner and suddenly, I was up against the wall, we were kissing passionately. I still compare every kiss to that one. The amount of pure lust and need he was giving off made me feel wanted in a way I have rarely felt since then. He asked me on a first date after that kiss in April and after the pizza we fooled around flirting with the idea of sex. But I wasn't ready and he was ok with that. We still talk a lot and hang out when we are in the same area. Last summer I went to an event with him and stayed over, finally having sex with him after we had known each other for four years. The next day when I was back in Santa Fe with my mom, she looked over at me and asked if my staying over had meant sex. I said yes. It was awkward, but I am glad that my parents and I have that relationship. I can admit to being a sexual person without them disowning or shaming me for it. If that man didn't want kids or was ever planning to leave that state, there is a part of me that would consider marrying him in a heart beat.

I had sex for the first time when I was nineteen and a Junior in college. The first real party of the year was going on and a freshman guy I was friends with and I had been flirting around the bonfire. I followed him to his dorm and we started to kiss and then slept together. I did not feel different. I felt normal. We never even went on a date. But what did that matter? I liked him. He liked me. We both wanted sex. We had condoms. And sex was a normal part of being an adult right?. It didn't even hurt because I was so into him and so ready. I had wanted to have sex for a while and just couldn't figure out how to make the decision. A part of me has never understood why people act like losing your v-card is such a huge deal.

But let me pause here for a moment because there is something that really struck me the day after I had sex. I felt normal but at the same time I couldn't help but wonder if something was wrong with me for feeling normal. I had this impression that it should have hurt. I should have felt different.

He should have been someone I loved. A girl's

virginity is a big deal right? I mean in some cultures

girls are checked for virginity before marriage. We

wear white at our wedding to represent virginity. So

shouldn't it be a bigger deal? Should I feel either

ashamed or awakened? But I felt neither. And then

it hit me why. I wasn't listening to myself when I

was questioning how I should feel, I was instead

listening to the world around me. I was raised to

believe that my body was mine. Masturbation and

sex were normal. When I was ready to have sex, I

could and should have sex. That night I was ready, I

was proactive about safety, and I was with a guy I

knew. Why should I feel weird or different just

because the world was telling me I should? The

answer was very simple. I shouldn't. That was the day I realized that I wasn't going to let anyone make me feel bad about sex or the way I had lost my virginity. I hadn't lost anything. I had simply started a new activity. I started driving at sixteen, voting at eighteen, and drinking at twenty-one but I never said I had lost something on those days. So why should starting to have sex mean I had lost something? In fact, did it not mean that I had gained something? I gained a new activity, a new way to feel, to connect.

I never lost my virginity, I started having sex.

I had my first serious boyfriend later that Junior year. He was sweet. We wasted no time before starting to sleep together and in a lot of ways it was a really good relationship. We weren't amazing in bed but it was still pretty good and we were safe and respectful when it came to boundaries and trying new things. That was when I started to get STD screens too just to be extra safe. I have never had any problems there. I had my first pregnancy scare that year, despite being good about my birth control. I was stressed and two weeks late. I didn't tell the boy because I didn't want him to panic. I called my mom and crying told her I was scared that I was pregnant. That is how she and my dad learned I was a sexually active adult. She was amazing.

"Calm down. You have been stressed out from school. Stress can make things late or not happen at all. Go buy a pregnancy test and take it. If it is negative then breathe and just accept that stress can do that to you. If it is positive then when I get back in town we will figure out what to do."

My dad echoed her in this matter. It was those reassuring words that made me realize everything would be ok. I knew my parents respected my not wanting kids anytime soon, and I knew that they respected my not ever wanting to be pregnant anytime soon either. If it was positive, my mom would help me get an abortion without judgement. I was twenty and my mom never once made me feel bad or stupid or pathetic for being afraid of being pregnant. And, in a way, that also meant she was in no way judging me for being a sexually active person. I breathed out a sigh of relief I did not know I had been holding since the day I slept with that guy at that party. For some reason I had thought my parents would judge me. After all the times they told me it was normal and healthy I still thought they would be judgmental. It sounds silly doesn't it?

By the time I graduated college, I had had a lot of firsts. A lot of new experience in the world of sex. Ever notice how until you finally do it, sex seems like the most mysterious thing in the world? It seems off limits. Adult. It feels dangerous and important and tempting and terrifying all at the same time. Everyone around you has different opinions about what sex is and what sex is for. One religion says it is only to have babies. Another that it is dirty if you do anything besides lie on your back with the man on top of you missionary style.

One person tells you that, because you are a girl, it's going to hurt and that terrifies you. The next person tells you it's fun and the best feeling ever. Then you watch porn because you want to see what it looks like and you start to wonder if you will be any good at it. Will you be loud like the girls in that porn? When I would pleasure myself I never wanted to be loud, would a guy change that? Even the simplest things seemed mysterious. When did you put the condom on? Did you help him or would he do it himself? So many questions. And every single person, book, and website tells you different things. And it isn't like I wanted to ask my parents more graphic details about sex. Like I said, before and even after that first time, sex is a mysterious and confusing world.

And now suddenly on the morning of that Halloween party, it had become even more confusing.

...Telling People...

"It was probably just a misunderstanding. Why don't we have him come in with you for your next session so you can hear his side of what happened?"

I woke up Sunday morning and knew I would have to tell people. Reddit had been no help. For every supportive message there were two like the ones you read earlier, dismissing my feelings and experience. I called my parents and told them. Crying. I felt like I had failed in some way. I did not want them to feel bad for me but I wanted my mommy. I wanted my papa. I still do almost every day. It has been four months and I still want to run home to my parents' house and just spend the rest of my life curled up in bed eating Chinese food and chocolate. They agreed to drive up the next weekend. Told me to keep going to school because of how hard I worked to get there. I do better when I am in school then when I am not doing anything.

I went to my therapy session Monday morning after skipping class. My therapist, a male, suggested I bring "my boyfriend" to a therapy session because the whole incident was just a misunderstanding, not an assualt. I left the office, angry. confused, needing confirmation of my own intuition. So I sent a text asking him if he would have continued with penetration if I hadn't woken up. He texted back, yes. I never went back to that therapist. How could a therapist undermine and dismiss my pain and confusion and act like it was all some superficial misunderstanding. His words made me feel so small. So stupid and pathetic. It was two days after that morning and I had yet to feel truly validated about my being assualted.

I drove back to school and asked to speak with the female Dean. She wasn't free, but the Dean of Student Affairs, was. He was the professor for one of my classes that semester. I was shaking trying not to cry as I told him what had happened. That I wasn't sure I could make it to every class that week. Some of my classes would be talking about laws around rape and women's' reproductive rights. Besides my parents, he was the only other person in that seventy- two hour period who had been completely understanding. He reassured me that he would email my professors and let them know I might be absent for a while. I had a personal problem that I was dealing with. He told me if I needed anything to just tell him. Told me not to worry about class too much and to focus on me.

I still tried to make it to a few classes that week. But every time I went to a class, I had an anxiety attack. I missed most of my classes that week. I would wake up wanting to go, but I would find myself unable to convince myself to shower. I had washed all my sheets so that the bed would smell clean. Why not just stay home? Part of me hated the outside world. Hated people.

My parents drove up on Saturday. After we spoke for a while we went out to eat. I acted strong. Talked about how I would stay in school. How I was ok. Sad and confused. But ok. I would be fine. I was fine. They stayed overnight and then left on Sunday.

I started having more problems and more confusing ways of solving them. I slept with a friend from school in a desperate attempt to make sure I could still have sex. I am still friends with him. Weirdly, that was the first time I felt normal. That was the only time I felt normal for a while. I started dating someone soon after. I needed some part of my life to feel normal. I had insomnia. My depression, anxiety, and PTSD, were aggravated more than they had ever been before. I was relying heavily on my Klonopin and Lexapro to feel even slightly ok for a few hours every day. I went to a few classes every week. Kept up with the readings, but did not really absorb any information.

Every single day part of me wanted to quit school. I wanted to curl up in a ball and hide away. I hated how confused I was about everything. I hated the way the world around me was so divided about what had happened to me. It sounds horrible, but there was a small part of me that wished I hadn't woken up in time to stop him. Wished he had been more violent. Maybe then I could quit school without argument or guilt. People would take me more seriously. I would know for sure. I could press charges — which I still have not done out of fear and confusion. People would understand my sudden desire to lie in bed all day without moving. I know it sounds horrible, I really do. But I want to be as honest as possible here.

...Four Months Later...

It has been four months since that morning. I am in therapy. I am still in law school. And I am participating in the school's rendition of *The Vagina Monologues*. But I have not fully recovered by any sense of the word. Sure I had a new relationship come and go. And I am continuing into my second semester of law school, but I don't feel normal. I can barely check my school email without severe anxiety. I feel nervous walking to school, walking alone even in my very small town. It takes a huge amount of effort to leave my house every day for classes, food, or social activities. I eat but not very regularly. If I forget to go buy food, I don't eat till the next day. I got sick a few weeks ago and so I have missed more classes. Not enough to be in trouble but still, I wanted to start the semester perfectly and that did not happen. I wanted to feel normal and unaffected, but that was probably an unrealistic expectation. I hate when people ask me what happened last semester that made me absent. Part of me wants to just come right out and say it. I was sexually assaulted. But the world around me implies that you don't just say that. The other part of me never wants to tell anyone. Too many people around me dismissed what happened. It was nonviolent. I was dating and sleeping with him. And I did not immediately try to stop him. He didn't even use force and eventually stopped. I was made to feel like that meant what happened was just a misunderstanding. My close friends, of course, understood, my Dean understood, my professors too. And my sex life didn't seem to be affected. In fact the only part of my life that feels normal is when I have sex. Sounds weird right? It was a sexual assault so how could sex feel normal when nothing else does? Honestly, I have no idea. Part of me thinks it was because I was so determined not to be the victim. I refused to let sex become scary or strange. But I was forgetting that no matter what, this attack would affect me. I did not even realize for a few weeks, how deeply I had been affected.

At first I only missed the classes dealing with rape and sexual assault for my Torts class. I had tried to go to the class the Monday right after and had a panic attack immediately after leaving the class. Then it started getting hard to leave in the mornings. Luckily, I had gone directly to my Dean and told him, so my absences were excused. But I started developing a fear towards my school email. Every time I missed a class, I thought that I would receive an email saying I was expelled. That is a fear I still have to this day. Every day I have two approaches to school, part of me wants to be kicked out so I can tell my parents at least I tried but obviously I need time to heal; but another part of me cares so much about succeeding here that I am so scared of failing I can't even check my email in case I already have. I read somewhere that anxiety and depression work together like this, "depression is never wanting to get up and go to class, anxiety is when you panic about failing because of that." Those are the two thoughts I battle with everyday on top of just not feeling well in everyday

situations. I simultaneously love being around

people and hate it at the same time. How weird does

that sound? Every time I talk about or have sex I

feel confident and fake at the same time. I feel like I

should have more trouble around sex. If the incident

affected me so much, shouldn't I have more trouble

in that area? But I don't. My therapist and the

RAINN website say that that is normal. That there

is no way to tell exactly how you will react, and no

reaction is wrong or strange. But my reaction makes

it harder to tell people. I live in fear that if I do tell

someone, they won't take me seriously. But I am

not writing all this down just to tell you what

happened to me. These words, this story has a

different purpose. I want to talk to you about the

way our culture talks about sex. About consent.

Because what I went through, what many women

go through and the way it was and is treated, just

can't continue to be acceptable. My experience was

dismissed due to the lack of violence involved.

Because the world I live in believes that if I am in a

sexual relationship with someone, I can never be

violated by them. But this won't change until we

take a hard look at the way we teach children and

teenagers about sex and about the feelings and

decisions that go with sex. This won't change until

we look at the gender roles that go into sex and

sexual relationships. Before I begin speaking more

intensely about these subjects, I want to give this

disclaimer:

I am a straight girl who has sex with men. I have only lived through the experiences given to me by that orientation and gender. So while I speak a bit about what guys experience, I am not an expert and this has to be understood when reading this work.

...Let's Talk Sex Ed...

Most schools give us a very basic version of
sexual education. The girls and boys are separated
and are told either by instructor or movie about
puberty, hormones, body changes, the basics of sex,
STDs, pregnancy, and condoms. The rest is left up
to the parents to teach. So every single person on
the planet has a different version of knowledge
about sex. And while I do respect different peoples'
right to educate their children how they want, there
are some problems that arise with such a varied
education. Part of these problems stem from the fact
that there is no country or worldwide regulations on
sex education. Even in America, where we like to
consider ourselves progressive, there are many

schools that do not teach sex education at all. And many, teach only abstinence. By the way, for a First World country, America has a fairly high teen pregnancy rate. I am not saying any one way is better and I don't have all the answers, but we have to admit to ourselves that there are problems.

My parents were both raised catholic. And for many Catholics sex ed is simple. Don't do it till marriage. There are even formal dances where daughters pledge their purity or abstinence to their fathers and receive rings to symbolize their vows. And while I agree that we should be allowed to choose when we want to have sex, I have heard a lot of stories of the negative affects of having abstinence only as an education. It ignores the out of control hormones most teens experience and leads to a fear for a lot of teens when they have a problem and want to get advice. It leads to shame if they make a mistake. It also leads to a lot of awkwardness, pain, and fear when the wedding night finally happens. If you had been told never to have sex and were so scared of disobeying this in any sense that you never tried to learn about sex, what would that first night look like? Would you know what a penis looks like? What to expect discomfort wise? Would you know about the importance of relieving yourself after to prevent infection? I have met quite a few people who would answer no to all of those questions. I am not saying this is true for all Catholics, and there are many religions where the same abstinence till marriage education is taught, but this is the religion I have had experience with and can speak to in a small way.

There are many cultures around the world where because of this abstinence education as well as misinformation, girls are examined for virginity before they are married. Those religions and cultures check for an undamaged hymen. But there is a very basic problem with this that education could solve. Hymens do not cover the whole vaginal opening, and are in fact easily torn by many activities. Sports, tampons, even just walking can tear the small rim of skin called a hymen. Some girls are born without hymens to begin with. So these exams may prove to these cultures that a girl is not a virgin when in fact, she has never had any sort of sexual contact. In some of these cultures, women are executed or shamed because they did not remain virgins when in fact they did. In many of these cultures if women are raped, she is either executed for extramarital sex or forced to marry her rapist to keep her family's honor.

There is no way to tell if a woman has had sex unless the sex was rough enough to lead to vaginal tearing. I want to repeat that: **There is no way to tell if a woman is a virgin or not. No way at all.**

My parents gave me a pretty inclusive sexual education. They were never concerned with what might happen if they exposed me to my body from a young age. Because it was my body and I saw it naked a lot. My mom taught me when I was old enough to wash myself to always make sure to wash my vagina. She never nicknamed it either.

Many parents will instead refer to private parts, the

downstairs area, flower, willy, pee pee. For my

brother and I it was always vagina and penis. For as

long as I can remember anyway. My mom taught

me how important it was to keep myself clean.

When I was older I was taught about condoms and

birth control, about masturbation as a way to relieve

feelings without having sex. About STDs and

testing. About going to see a gynecologist when I

became sexually active. They taught me that it was

ok to think about sex and be curious about it. But

that did not stop me from having fears. When I

wanted to start birth control I was scared because

girls around me spoke about their parents refusing

to help them. Some of them had stories about when

their parents found birth control in their rooms and became so enraged, that these girls were grounded for months. When I had that pregnancy scare, I was terrified and ashamed to tell my mom, despite my parents telling me I could always come to them without fear or shame, because of the hundreds of stories about girls being cut off or thrown out of the house because their pregnancy proved they were having sex. I get tested regularly for STDs and buy condoms when I need to, and despite that meaning I am doing everything right, I still feel a twinge of shame when in front of a cashier or doctor. My parents did everything possible to raise me without fear or shame around my body and sex but the world around me is so strong, so influential that I cannot help but feel negatively about the fact that I am a sexually active adult.

There is of course a double standard here that is part of the reason I can't help but feel bad about sex. And it isn't my imagination. Some schools and videos even demonstrate this as a part of sexual education. That old video of a guy and girl on their wedding night is a pretty good example. He holds up her dirty old sneakers and tells her how disgusting they are. That they look like the whole football team had put their feet in these sneakers. It wasn't less disgusting because she had made sure they all wore socks. The euphemism was very clearly demonstrating that it was gross that she had had sex before even when she had used a condom with each encounter. It is a double standard all women feel from puberty on. Books, television, media, and even jokes and conversation indicate that there is a strong difference between men who have sex and girls. Women who have lots of sex are "used up." The language gets even more disturbing. Some of the things I have heard as a female, starting from puberty, even before I was sexually active, include;

"If you have too much sex your pussy will be loose and no guy will want to have sex with you."

"Guys can have sex but you shouldn't. You are a girl and no guy wants to have sex with a girl who's had other dicks inside her."

"If you don't put out no guy will ever want to date you. But if you put out too much, why would a guy want to date you?"

Then there are the hundreds of jokes you hear every day about girls.

"What is loud and obnoxious? A woman."

"What do you call a woman who can't make sandwiches? Single"

"What do you call a girl who doesn't give head? You don't?"

These are just a few of the many, many jokes about women I heard every day in middle and high school. Imagine hearing things like that everyday while you are growing up dealing with hormones. And it is not just guys. The girls in my middle school during gym would sing this song,

"Stop, don't touch me there. This is my private square. R-A-P-E, Get your penis out of me."
In a sing song happy voice. It was a funny joke. I

always found it disturbing. The boys would laugh when the girls started singing it.

On top of this, the school had dress codes. It mostly concerned girls and what we could or could not wear. Yoga pants, spaghetti straps, and showing bra straps were all not allowed. Many schools have this dress code and many give the reason that it is distracting to boys. So I got the impression that it was my job to worry about how I was coming across to men. It wasn't about whether I was comfortable or not. It was about how my appearance would affect the men in my class. Going braless was looked down upon because your boobs would be bouncy and catch attention. This is a lesson, most if not all, girls hear from middle school on. It is your job to not be distracting. This leads to a culture where you start hearing, *"What did you expect, wearing such a short skirt?"*

Victim blaming. I have heard it. You have heard it. We have all heard it.

"She was drinking."

"She knew they were untrustworthy."

"She walked alone in a bad neighborhood."

"She was wearing a sexy, revealing outfit."

When I was assaulted I was told that it wasn't real because I had let him sleep in bed next to me naked. That it wasn't real because I had a sexual relationship with him. I was made to feel that because of that, my body belonged to him. He could do anything he wanted to me sexually because I had already let him touch me consensually. It made me feel like after sex, nothing he could do to me surrounding sex would be wrong. But what do these situations have to do with our sexual education? I think everything. We cannot have a conversation about sexual education without talking about consent.

Last year, in twenty-fifteen, California became the first state to require sexual consent lessons in high school. Why is this so important? Because consent is a very broad, very grey area of sex, and it shouldn't be. Healthy sexual relationships are based on both parties agreeing to having a sexual relationship. And here is where it gets complicated, there are different ways to consent and nobody can agree on how much consent needs to be given or what type of lack of consent constitutes non consent. I was told that until I told him no, my assaulter was not committing assault. Sure his hand was inside me, but I hadn't yet said no.

Here is the problem with this; we had had conversation on sexual fantasies and discussed what we wanted to try before. Sex while I was asleep had never come up. If that was something he wanted, should he not have brought that up when we discussed handcuffs, toys, and even the possibility of anal? I gave him every opportunity to mention this to me. I don't think it's fair for the man I'm sleeping with, to test out a new fantasy without asking me first. The moment he realized that he wanted to have sex with me while I was asleep, he should have woken me up, had a conversation with me, asked permission to engage in sex while I was asleep, and then respected whatever decision I gave him. Instead he tried something new, forcing me into a position where I had to ask myself: what do I do to make this stop ?And there was no easy answer. You might say, of course there is. Just push him away. Say no. But I couldn't just say no. I was frozen. Incapable of moving air over vocal chords. What if this new sexual experience that he was trying without me meant he was willing to go farther.?To push me down to finish the job. To kill me because I resisted. I never said no to him until the fear of actually being penetrated by his penis overpowered the fear of him becoming forceful. And I really only managed that because I needed the moment to be over so much, that I was willing to risk him becoming violent, risk him killing me if necessary to end it. Because I never ever said yes to him fondling me so intimately or engaging in sex while I was asleep. I never would have. If we had spoken openly about this particular subject, I would have told him that if he woke up and was horny, he wake me up. Kiss my cheek and whisper to me until I was awake. Shake me awake if necessary. Masturbate if he was really that blue balled. But putting part of himself inside me without my conscious presence, that is not something I ever would have agreed to. I am not even sure I would have felt comfortable with him french kissing me with his tongue inside my mouth while I am asleep. And I never got the chance to express any of that. I never had the option.

One of the responders on the advice post I put up told me that I should have told him before hand that that was a boundary for me. But no one ever told me that a guy I trusted, might try to have sex with me while I was asleep. Try to wake me up for sex maybe, but not actually have sex with me while I was unconscious. Why was I the one who was supposed to bring it up? It was not my fantasy. Should I and every girl expect that a guy will try this and bring it up first?Is that not victim blaming? Is that not putting all the expectations on the person the act is done unto? To anyone who says yes, I should have told him no before it happened I have only one thing to say to you:

Unless he tells me that that is something he is into, how the hell was I supposed to know to tell him I don't want it done to me? You are part of the problem.

Every single person who has ever thought or said that we should have known better, whether it is about clothing, drinking, location, or behavior is part of the problem. Only one person is ever to blame for an assault or rape, **the attacker**. I would go as far as saying the culture and lack of consent education is at fault too, but at the end of the day, it is always the attacker's fault. But to more fully understand my point about my situation in context of sexual education, we must return to the idea of consent.

...Consent and Conversations...

Let us return to the discussion of consent. Consent is defined by most as, *giving permission for something to happen.* Sounds simple doesn't it? Apparently not. Consent, when it comes to sex, is one of the most complicated subjects I have ever tried to research, learn, talk about, and understand. Not one person, book, media source, or educational group has the same answer. And while I don't have the solution for how we should approach consent, I think we need to start having more open and serious discussions regarding consent. I think no matter what religion, context, or personal preference we come from, we should all be willing to have a conversation on consent. Because we live in a world where I was made to feel bad or wrong about what happened to me. Because I live in a world where I am made to feel like an entirely sexual object that men have every right to make sexual advancements on, no matter the situation. Because I live in a world where half of the people I've encountered, told me that I should have known to say no before I was given the option to say yes. Because I wasn't even given the option to consent.

Consent is a grey area for most of us. We are told that if you drink alcohol and are drunk you cannot give consent, yet so many hookups happen in bars or at parties between two intoxicated parties that we almost never come across people who would actually consider themselves assaulted. And when both people are intoxicated can we really consider it nonconsensual for either party?

At my college one semester a guy got in trouble because he and a girl had hooked up while drunk. The story went that they had both had a lot to drink and had retired to his room, she had told him she would not sleep with him but after an hour of making out told him to go get a condom and put it on. They had sex and the next morning she told her friend she regretted the encounter. It eventually reached the administration and suddenly, he was facing accusations of rape. He was never charged, but he was kicked out of school because he had provided alcohol and she was not of drinking age. Because somehow, he had been accused of rape.

Because consent is a grey area we do not know how to talk about.

Go on reddit.com and find the subreddit on sex. There are hundreds of posts talking and asking about consent and how to discuss boundaries, fantasies, and fetishes. Hundreds of posts about whether my boyfriend, girlfriend, husband,wife, lover, or friend had crossed a boundary and how to handle it. Sex is something everyone has heard of, most people have, and yet, no one seems to know how to talk about it.

The difference between how girls and guys speak about sex or are spoken to about sex is part of the confusion. How can we expect to have a real conversation about sexual education and consent, without also acknowledging that the way we approach sex differs greatly depending on gender.?

Men seem allowed to speak openly about their

"conquests," where girls are far more timid and

concerned about sharing sexual exploits out of fear

of being called names. This is part of the reason I

love Amy Schumer as an actress, comedian, and

role model. She is open sexually. Makes jokes about

her many conquests and refuses to be shamed for

talking openly about such subjects. But due to this

many people, many men, find her unfunny,

inappropriate, and brash. But men talk about their

bodies, their girlfriends, and their sex without end

and nobody even blinks twice. The word dick enters

into every day conversation every single day.

Locker room talk is considered so normal it has a

name. Men can casually laugh together about that

blonde bimbo they banged last night. That red-haired chick who was totally crazy in bed. The brunette yoga instructor who could flex into new and exciting positions. Every day you here some sort of joke, conversation, or comment about sex from some guy or media outlet or show.

Have you ever really thought about strip clubs? The majority, at least the majority that you hear about, are girls entertaining men. Have you ever really thought about porn? When you hear conversation about those two professions, the women are thought of negatively, and the men are just ignored or applauded. It is normal for a guy to go to a strip club and watch porn. It is disgusting and demeaning for a woman to be a stripper or porn actress. Prostitution is the oldest profession, but prostitutes are dirty and you should not touch them with a ten foot pole. Because men can and should have sex, but the women they have sex with are whores. So how do we start to address these differences and the problems they create? And really what does gender have to do with consent? To answer these questions, we must return to speaking about the nature of sex, and examine how children, teenagers, and adults are introduced to the world of sex.

...Your Baby is going to Have Sex...

Human nature and the nature of civilizations will always lend themselves toward grey areas. What may look simple or black and white, often reveals itself to be a grey area when examined further. The question of murder is a good example. Most would say, murder is bad. It is that simple. But there is a famous example of where this becomes more complicated. Five people are on a train track unable to move as a train barrels toward them unable to stop. You are on a bridge with another individual. If you push this individual off the bridge and in front of the train, they will die and the the other five will live. So do you sacrifice one life for five? What if the five on the track are children? Or the one on the bridge is a child? What would go into your decision?

Sex, and every decision and question surrounding it, is so filled with grey areas, that at times it feels like attempting to diffuse a bomb. With a hundred same colored wires. And the fate of the whole world depends on you succeeding. Now don't get me wrong, I in no way believe that sex will ever be just black and white. But I do think that it warrants an ongoing ever-evolving conversation.

The conversation, can and should start as early as childhood. I'm not a parent, but I do know that when you become a parent, however it happens, it is your job to prepare your child for the adult world they will eventually become a part of. And you may not want to think about their future sex life, but unless they are asexual or disinterested in sex for other reasons, eventually that baby is going to grow up, feel the raging hormones and lust, and want to release those feelings, through sex. As the parent it is your job to make sure that when they become adults, they become capable of healthy sexual relations with themselves and others. Relying only on the school sex ed that many of us go through and many more do not, just is not enough. It leads to us, as teenagers, searching for information from friends, the internet, movies, and books. And that leads to us having a lot of misinformation, a lot of awkwardness, pain, discomfort, and an inability to have the healthiest sex possible. You can't claim that your religion teaches abstinence so you are the exception. That little girl or boy will get married eventually and then sex is allowed right? Just because it may not happen earlier doesn't mean you get a free pass to not teach your kid about something that will eventually be a part of their life. Teach your son that there is no such thing as a hymen so if he doesn't feel a "barrier" on their first night, it doesn't mean she lied about her virginity. Teach your daughter that after sex she has to pee or she could get an infection. Teach both genders that when you respect the person you are with sex can be a painless fun way to strengthen your intimacy and bond. But don't use your religion as an excuse to ignore the fact that eventually sex will enter that kid's life whether after marriage or before.

I had a conversation once with a woman who had had her son circumcised at birth and was very proud of this. The family was not Jewish, there had been no medical need, but because in America, male circumcision is a reflex, she had had it done. Her baby, her choice, almost as if he was her newest doll. I asked her during this conversation whether she had considered the possible future risks for her son and she told me there were no risks. This is not true at all. Men who are "cut" as we call it can have feelings of betrayal towards their parents. They can experience a loss of function and/or sensation. And these are just two of many possible risks. So I asked this woman if she had known about these possible risks to her son and she answered no. Then I asked her how she would feel if when her son grew up and began to have relationships including sexual ones, and was not able to feel pleasure or function. Her response shocked me.

"I am not thinking about his future sex life. It is not of my concern as his mother."

I get it. I really do. Sex is not something we are raised to believe parents and kids should talk about openly. You don't share details about your sexual history with your parents and we consider it gross or embarrassing when we see are parents kiss or we accidentally walk in on them in the throws. But that does not mean as a parent you can ignore that sex will be a part of that kid's life. Imagine that that baby boy becomes a teenager. He is seventeen, has a girlfriend he loves or likes, and the two of them decide to take the relationship to the next level. All their friends talk about how good it feels. Television and movies go on and on about this orgasmic experience. So they get to it, and he feels nothing. He comes to find out that his nerves were damaged because the circumcision was imperfect. Imagine if that kid were to ask his mom why he was cut and whether she had considered this result. And he hears this answer;

"I was not thinking about your future sex life. It is not my concern as your mother."

I don't know about you, but If my mom ever said something like that about any part of my life, even the sexual part, I would feel destroyed. Betrayed. I would be angry and horrified. I might never speak to her again. But that is our culture. On one side, sex is shown as fun and incredible, but on the other side, sex is seen as embarrassing, disgusting, and not something we talk about in polite company. We shouldn't tell our teens or kids about sex because it is an adult issue. But that view point fails to recognize your duty as the parent to prepare your kid for adult life. For every part of their future adult life. But we don't. Instead we just try not to think about our kids as being sexual despite this leaving them completely unprepared for even the simplest of sexual experiences.

During one of my first sexual experiences, I was with a guy who was having trouble getting hard. That is normal, it happens. But when we were first naked together he was very small. He was maybe one inch. I will admit, I was a bit disappointed. I started to lose my arousal. But I continued to kiss him because I didn't want to hurt his feelings. Well when he got more into it, he grew. A lot. Guess what the school sex ed had left out? Now I hear it all the time. Girls talk about their sexual encounters and one question that comes up is whether he was a "grower or shower." I have heard stories where girls have ditched a sexual situation because of what was there when he wasn't quite in the mood yet, ignoring the possibility that he was a grower and would grow, when more relaxed and in the mood. I am not saying that is wrong or right, and it certainly is not very nice to the guy, but that is what happens when you don't teach girls anything about real life penises. Teenage males need to learn more about their own penises as well. I see it everywhere, guys are constantly obsessed with whether they are considered big. Here at least, the average is about five inches. Less than two is considered a micro penis. But the truth is, it really depends on your partner during a specific encounter whether your penis is a decent size. Some girls are smaller and tighter, some a bit bigger and looser. Some women hate having too much penis inside them, and some need the massive monster penises you hear about in porn and erotica. Just like some men prefer the feel of one woman's vagina to another. Women too need to learn more about their own vaginas. Where the clit, pee hole, and actual vaginal passage are and to expect that various things and people will feel different. We are all designed differently so we prefer different things sexually. But we are not told that ever. Not until we are actually thrown into the world of sex and start researching it for ourselves. Even then, you get some mixed messages about whether you can get over sexual incompatibility or not.

I also did not know what a cut versus uncut penis looked like. Did not know that it was normal for the penis's function to depend on the day, the amount of alcohol involved, and even just how tired someone is. And that actually goes for both genders. My vagina has been known to shut down because of fatigue, alcohol, or even because my bed made a weird noise that one time. Those were all things I only learned through having sex with different guys and starting to talk to my friends and doing research on the internet. The sheer amount of other girls who knew nothing about the male anatomy, their own anatomy, and how they might work or not work, is incredible.

The sad thing about this, of course, is that this lack of knowledge does not just effect us, it effects the guys we like too. It affects our relationships. So many feelings of inadequacy on both ends because he couldn't get it up one night, or he lost it another. Half of me would blame him for not knowing how to use his own body, half of me would think it was my fault. I wasn't good looking enough, did not know enough about sex to know how to keep him hard. But no, he was just tired and stressed that day.

The reverse is true as well. Girls get aroused too. But our bodies don't always work perfectly either. I can't count the number of times I have really liked a guy or was dating a guy, and I was in the mood, but my body was like, *no, not today, maybe tomorrow.* Was I broken? What was I doing wrong? I could see the feelings of failure in the man's eyes as he thought that maybe it was his fault. But no, I was just stressed out or had had a cider.

These are not uncommon stories either. Almost every person I have ever spoken to about sex has experienced a failure to thrive down there. And almost every person has had an experience where they were made to feel as though that failure was something to feel ashamed of. It happens to everyone so why do we consider it such an embarrassment? Education. Or in reality, the lack of education is responsible. I'm not saying that parents or schools should go into graphic detail, but would it really be so harmful to mention some of these complexities?

We do not even have to start the conversations with the nitty gritty sex details, just teaching about how to be respectful to other people would help later in the more awkward sexual situations.

We need to start these conversations in childhood. Even just start by teaching the basics of respect for yourself and others. Sounds simple right? But we all know toddlers and kids who have less than zero respect for the world around them. This might change and get better, but if it doesn't can you imagine what this kid will look like in a relationship? In sex? There is no excuse for not teaching a kid the basics of respect. Not only would it help them later in love but it will help them make friends, contacts, and succeed in all parts of life. Empathy too would help in these ways. Teach your kid that those people are people too. Do unto others as you would have done unto you. Sound familiar? We need to teach something else too. Ask first. There are many who say: *"it is easier to ask forgiveness than it is to ask permission."* I say to that, What the hell is wrong with you? It may be easier, but that doesn't make it the better option. My assaulter followed that modem of thought and as the victim, I can tell you I should have been asked permission first. In most situations, it should not be what is easier, it should be what is better, what is more respectful? Is the easier option for you, victimizing or harming someone else?

When you make decisions, you need to know and understand that you are not alone in the world. Of course we can't possibly care about how our actions might affect all seven billion people, I am not saying that. But in situations like sex, you have to consider how your decisions directly impact your partner. Because your feelings are not more important than hers or his. There is not one person on this planet who deserves respect, pleasure, and empathy more than another. My world revolves around me, yours around you, and that is normal. But when your world and my world collide we cannot use our egos to justify harming each other. You cannot say that your world matters more than mine because the moment you say that, you are negating me and my world as having as much right to exist. I'm not talking about whether I contribute as much to this world as you or whether murders and pedophiles should have the same basic rights. Those are conversations for a different type of book. I am talking about stripping away everything but our basic humanity.

When you and I are standing naked looking into each others eyes, your pleasure, your needs, and your wants are not more important than mine. There is nothing in this world that can justify you satisfying your world by harming mine. Because at the end of it all, I am not white, atheist, middle class, young, red haired, or a victim. I am human. And so are you.

My assailant woke up horny and, whether consciously or subconsciously, he made a decision that morning that his needs mattered more than my bodily autonomy. My body was there to satisfy his needs. My needs did not even exist in that moment. He was not trying to wake me up. He was not trying to bring my conscious mind into the equation. And my conscious mind is what make me, me. What makes me human. And in that moment I was not human, I was a fleshlight. That's how it felt at least. Is this beginning to make sense yet? Maybe all of this could have been avoided if kids were more exposed to how respect and empathy play into exploration of their bodies and the bodies of others.

We have to teach kids about their bodies. Not just basic anatomy, but we need to tell them it is normal and ok for things to feel certain ways and for them to explore their bodies. Just maybe don't do that in public and don't do it to another person. That would be disrespectful. I'm not saying teach your kid how to masturbate or go into graphic details about sex, but stop acting like the first time your kid will notice her clit or his penis is the magic age of puberty which, by the way, can start as early as nine. There is a great episode of the television show *House*, where a mother brings her toddler to the clinic because the kid is making these weird noises and body movements. House in his sarcastic and rude way eventually tells the mom with several euphemisms that her toddler is, in fact, masturbating. And the mother is just horrified. She covers her daughter's ears, and gets defensive, even offended. This is how most parents would react. Their precious child is innocent, has never been abused, has no reason to touch themselves. But why would that kid who crawls around touching everything in the room, putting everything in its mouth, why would that same kid not explore their own body? It is ignorant, naive, and even harmful to refuse to acknowledge that that is a possibility. That kid has all the body parts it's going to have when puberty hits. Hormones are added to the equation which of courses changes the way the kid thinks and acts about his/her body. The kid's emotions change too. The body changes in some ways but nothing is subtracted. Yes the body gains some hair in new places, some fat in others. But the penis, vagina, and clit have always been there to be touched and explored. Do you really think that kid has never noticed his or her own body? Didn't Freud say something about kids having sexual impulses? Not in the same way as teens and adults, but still.

There are parents who are ready to admit they have caught there young kids exploring those lower body parts, but not many will go farther then just telling the kid not to do that. Why are we stopping kids from being curious about themselves? Why not just tell them that while exploring their body is normal, it is something to be done in private and alone. Of course some may also say that it is normal for kids to explore with other kids too, but as I am not educated in child development I am not going to speak to that. I just know enough to know that at least by themselves, it is normal and healthy for kids to self explore. Teach them not to explore in public, but don't make them feel like it is wrong to notice their own body. That's how whole body shame and fear of nudity starts. Continuing with this thought, teach kids not to feel shame towards their bodies. Everyone has a body, so why are we teaching kids to feel embarrassed about their bodies? Yes, in public we have to wear clothes, but in private encourage kids to get naked and look at themselves. Teach them that everyone has a body. That every body while slightly different has pretty much the same parts. Teach boys while they are kids that it is normal for their penises to move and harden so that when it happens for the first time they do not panic. Teach girls that their vaginas can get wet and that it may bleed at some point in the future. Periods can start earlier than you think so make sure they know before hand that it could happen, it is normal, and it is in fact healthy. If we teach kids to be respectful of their own bodies, maybe that would help them learn how to respect the bodies of others as they grow from kids to teenagers.

Could you imagine a world where all of us grew up feeling secure? At least about our bodies and our curiosity towards them? These are the first few steps toward a healthy sexual education. Teach respect and teach bodies and teach how the two go hand in hand. Kids need to know these things. They aren't stupid and they can handle it.

…Your Teenager is Going to have Sex…

That kid has now grown up and hits puberty. All of a sudden. It happened so fast didn't it?The game changes permanently. Their bodies are changing and their hormones are rampaging through their bodies faster than the speed of light. And neither you nor that kid is ready. Sounds familiar doesn't it? If you aren't a parent, you have heard the parents around you talk about that kid. Or you were that kid. I was that kid twelve years ago. I got my period early at eleven. And life changed very quickly after that. I cared a whole lot more about my clothes, about the opinions of boys, and hated my new monthly ritual of pain and blood. Also I got horny. Extremely horny. Like in every dream I had and in every daydream, I imagined sex, sex, and lots more sex.

By the way, most teenagers are obsessed with sex, with their bodies, and with the bodies of those they are attracted to. Some are obsessed with all bodies not just those of the people they get the tingles for. Have you spent any considerable time around teens? The jokes, everyday conversation, and even insults all have mentions of sex. But this is highly ignored. We teach kids the basics. Boy parts, girl parts, pregnancy, STD, condoms,. But then it is up to the parents to fill in the gaps. For me this leaves far to much up in the air. Parents have their own ideas about when their kids should have sex. But not every teen agrees and even if the teen at first agrees with their parent, life happens. This becomes problematic of course because neither the

teen nor the parent wants to talk about sex. They

don't want to admit to the other that sex exists, so

you end up with a teen who has no idea how to get

birth control but still wants sex and is going to have

sex, but who is also too scared to admit to their

parents that they are going to have sex because

mom and dad said not to do it. And then of course

you get shame, fear, and in the worse case

scenarios, STDs and pregnancy. All of this without

mom and dad ever knowing that you are terrified of

everything happening with you and your sex partner

so suddenly you have a fifteen year old who is six

months pregnant past the point of abortion and who

has not been taking the right vitamins or seeing a

doctor enough to be sure they are healthy. Do you see how quickly this spiraled out of control?

Parents and guardians; that teenager is her or his own person. Scary right? Their bodies are changing, but so are their minds, wants, and desires. We become rebellious as teens. I was horrible to my own mom at thirteen. And fourteen. And fifteen. We got into screaming matches entirely instigated because I was a lazy, depressive, teen who stopped caring about homework. It wasn't her fault. My hormones made me feel so weird and school was so terrible for me that I couldn't help but not want to do any work. And I took it out on my parents but mostly on my mom. This comes with the territory of teenagers. We stop listening, think we know better than anyone else, and while we get into trouble due to these changes, this is an important part of our development. We need to learn how to stand on our own two feet. Make our own decisions and watch those decisions lead to very epic failures. Part of this new need to be our own persons, is making decisions about our bodies. Of course some things become legal issues because teens are immature, have undeveloped brains, and are not adults. You cannot get pierced or tattooed under eighteen and that is probably for the best. If you are older than eighteen you cannot have sex with someone under the age of consent of that location because of the authority and pressure teens feel from older individuals. But we cannot make all sex illegal until a certain age because we could not enforce that in the first place and we would be ignoring basic human biology as well the science behind puberty itself. Sure some people wait and not everyone in the world has sex or wants sex, but we cannot ignore the fact that in general, teenagers start experimenting sexually when puberty hits. Making out, oral sex, using fingers, and sometimes, yes, even full penetrative sex. Parents cannot just cop out of this reality. You cannot hide behind, *"I taught them better than that,"* or *"she pledged abstinence because she loves her father and God."* You cannot force your opinions, your wants, and your desires onto your kids. Especially not about something as personal as sex. It isn't healthy. And it just is not realistic.

We need to teach teenagers not to fear asking us about sex. They need to have someplace safe to go to learn about sex and relationships without it becoming a cultural or religious problem. Without making them feel like failures for even just asking questions. Because let's face it teens do not always listen to parents. In fact, the majority of the time, they actively try not to listen. You have every right to tell them how you feel and what you want, but you do not get to force them to obey your orders. At least not about sex. Because that kid who is so scared to ask you questions about such a huge part of life, is the kid who is going to end up in a bad situation because they don't know the difference between what's normal and what isn't. That is the kid who is going to end up with Aids or pregnant because they could not even ask you about sex and protection. Isn't that possibility worse than just admitting that your kid might go and have sex behind your back? Would it not be better to at least prepare them for that possibility? You can tell them that you would rather they wait, warn them about the emotional and physical dangers and complexities that begin when sex joins your world. But just saying no and leaving it at that, who is that really helping? Your kid, or you?

I was twenty when I had a pregnancy scare. And I cannot imagine trying to handle a pregnancy scare on my own if I had been too afraid to tell my parents. And I was still a bit scared. I mean the world around me made it seem like if I was pregnant at that age I had to have failed in some way. It ignored that birth control can fail. It just can. It ignored that periods can be late and that leads to a lot of scares. Especially by young girls who don't know how periods work or don't have enough information to know that oral sex doesn't really lead to babies. But my parents didn't have rules about when I could have sex or not. If they had, I would have faced the most horrifying moment in my life without support from the two people who mattered most. The two I relied on in every crisis I had ever faced before. Could you imagine not being able to go to the people who helped you when you were young and got scraped and bruised? Who helped you do homework and taught you right from wrong? We rely on our parents to help us handle these situations, but some of us can't rely on our own parents to help them in a bad sex situation.

That is the world we live in. And if you can excuse my language, that sucks. A lot.

We need to help teenagers learn the truths about the world of sex. Condoms can break. That's what Plan b is for and why it is becoming more and more accessible. We should encourage teens to explore their sexuality in a healthy safe way. Tell them that masturbation is ok. It is how you learn about your body and what it wants. Maybe teach girls about vibrators. That might be the most awkward conversation ever, but vibrators are why I didn't have sex till I was nineteen. I could handle all of my horniness in my room. By myself. When you start dating, it's ok to be confused as hell. To stumble around blindly. Kissing is fun. Everyone does it and you shouldn't feel weird about having the urge to kiss someone you like, and if they kiss back, Yay! If not, that is ok too. They don't have to like you or kiss you back just because you like them. Let it go. Walk away. When you want to fool around with someone, try to be safe. It is better to use condoms even for blowjobs, not that everyone does but it would be safer. Start getting tested for STDs if you are going to be having any type of sex. That way if you go ahead and do something without a condom, since we all have our stupid moments, you know whether you or not you are safe and you can make sure you are not going to give someone some infection without realizing it. That's why free clinics exist. And it is why we need parents to wake up a bit, smell the awkward sex roses, and deal with them. You decided to be a parent and you can't just not parent them when it comes to sex. You cannot pick and choose where you parent.

PSA ANNOUNCEMENT: If your teen is too scared to tell you that they are having sex because of your attitude towards them and sex, and your teen gets an infection, I don't really blame the kid if it spreads. That teenager doesn't handle the insurance and there might not be a free clinic near by. If they can't find a way to get to a doctor because the only way is through you and that is a horrifying and deadly concept to them, you are failing your kid and any kid they go and sleep with. It may sound harsh, but so is gonorrhea.

There is this episode in the show *Private Practice* that demonstrates this point explicitly. This kid is like fourteen and tells his doctor that he has a girlfriend and is ready to have sex with her. Unbeknownst to him, he was born HIV Positive and his parents have not gotten around to telling him. The pediatrician is trying to convince him to wait and the parents to fess up because it isn't the boy who is at risk here, it is whichever girl he is about to sleep with, but he can't break patient confidentiality or disobey the parents. The next day the pediatrician finally in desperation just blurts out to the parents that the kid wants sex and is about to have sex. The parents are forced to come clean and the episode ends with the kid tearfully telling the pediatrician that it was too late. Sex had happened the night before.

This fictional kid and parents were so incapable of talking to each other about sex, that a third party, an innocent girl, was unknowingly exposed to a very dangerous virus. This may be a fictional example, but I bet anything something similar happens all the time in real life. How could it not?

Teenagers are going to have sex. They just are. So lets teach them about the different types of birth control available so they can take charge of their sexual health. Let's teach them how to talk about sex with adults who can help them get what they need. Let's teach parents how to accept that their wants for their teens are not always the reality of what the teens are going to do. We cannot just throw them into adult hood and expect the answers to pop up at the exact right times. I knew about birth control pills for years before I actually wanted them, but at least I knew I could ask, that I wouldn't just be relying on condoms when I finally did want to have sex. Because my parents were willing to accept that I was a person, with hormones, that was going to want sex. But beyond just teaching parents and kids how to talk about sex, we also need to teach teenagers about consent and respect in relation to sexual relationships because that is how we ensure that they will not have twisted ideas on what is allowable and appropriate in sexual situations. In order to teach the younger generations, we first have to have a conversation with ourselves and the people around us of every age about sex, consent, and the grey areas we are all going to face.

...The Conversations We Need...

It sounds easy. Girl and boy meet. Or boy and boy. Or girl and girl. Or whatever combination you can think of. They like each other and at some point the clothes come off. Sweating, noises, and nakedness fill the room. Then it's done. Maybe you cuddle, get food, or maybe one person just gets dressed and leaves. The problem is, sex is both the easiest and most natural activity in the world and the hardest, most complicated, and frustrating situation we face.

Take me for example. I was born a girl and I like guys. I really like guys. I am in my twenties and I've had both meaningful relationships and one night stands. I have had good sex, bad sex, frustrating sex, and "oh my god yes" sex. I masturbate regularly, have watched porn, spoken with lots of friends and just people about sex, and I have had the let's try everything once type of sex. In my opinion, I have had a pretty well rounded sex life. But even I run into very confusing situations.

I dated a guy recently who was fairly new to sex. We were kissing and had gotten to the point where we were no longer wearing shirts, he was hard and I was very very ready to do the naked hokey pokey with him. So trying to make sure that this new sex rookie was ok I asked him if he wanted to have sex. He answered with, *" I mean if you want to we can."* Do you have any idea how confusing that answer was? His tone of voice didn't help either. He didn't sound super enthused, but he didn't sound upset or scared or uncomfortable either. We spent ten minutes playing the naked do you want to chicken dance.

"I don't want to make you uncomfortable. If you want to have sex we can but if you don't just tell me. It is ok."

"I mean yeah if you want to then I am ok with doing it."

This kept going. For ten minutes. We eventually did get to the sex portion of the evening when he finally went to the bathroom, came back, and was so into the moment that we didn't speak words until he had gotten the condom on, pushed me down, and the sex was in full go mode. But before that, the situation was confusing as hell. His yes for sex wasn't really a yes. It sounded like a, *"I guess I will if you want to.*" It made me feel like I was putting pressure on him when that was not my intention at all.

I ended up breaking up with this same guy because after almost a month and a half, the guy had no ability to recognize my sexual needs or make any effort to satisfy them. We would speak openly about sex and possible wants or fantasies, but he would get very shy, very uncomfortable talking about it. Here was a twenty-three year old male who somehow had zero ability to even speak about sex without immediate embarrassment. I can't judge him for that, I don't know his past, but it made it very hard for me to know how to proceed in the relationship. This boy opened my sex box to grab a condom and when he saw my vibrator, he giggled, closed the box quickly, and could not look me in the eyes. It made me feel ashamed for a moment, embarrassed even. His inability to speak about sex with me, the person he was getting naked with, caused a lot of frustration on my end. It was an especially weird sexual relationship because of his inability and unwillingness to touch anything during the act. We would be in the moment and, because it happens a lot, his penis would slip out. Ok the normal situation here is one of us grabs the penis and puts it back in. This boy never wanted to touch himself during the act. He never once tried to reach down to adjust himself back in. He would also never try to touch my body during it. He fingered me once in two months and never even attempted to go down on me. Not for lack of me trying either. I mean I tried to tell him that it would be nice if this happened. But no, it never did.

And he was not very delicate when I went down on him. I get that sometimes when you are uncomfortable, we say things we don't mean, but this was just uncalled for. He had been drinking and was very tired. We were lying in bed and he told me to look down. He was hard, ok. He started to just look at himself and then at me and finally just gestured with his hands that I should go down on him. I did for a few minutes, we had some sex, but he wanted to finish with me giving him oral. It became very clear after twenty minutes that he was not going to release, whether due to the drinking or the fatigue. He even tried to finish himself for a few minutes to no avail. And that is ok. It happens. We all have sex without the happy ending at some

point. But after another twenty minutes of me trying

with hands and mouth because he kept encouraging

me, he sighed and said in an irritated tone,

"Well I guess I just won't ever cum again."

I should have said something, but it felt like

I had been punched in the gut. I left for a few

minutes to go to the bathroom, but it was really so I

wouldn't cry in front of him. I couldn't even

understand how he could think that would sound

good to hear. After trying for almost an hour, After

even he had tried. I am so sorry that for once you

did not get off! This was a guy who couldn't even

look at my vibrator without acting offended, would

not touch or go down on me, would not even

attempt any of the sexual or even just kissing

techniques I had mentioned to him that made me feel good, but he had the audacity to be insulting because that one night he couldn't get off. Pardon again my language, but that is seriously fucked up. I cannot even be polite about that anymore.

Let me tell you about the "straw that broke the camels back" experience I had with him. I finally told him that I wanted to hear about his possible wants in the sex department in a final attempt to improve our sex life. I like furry handcuffs, what did he like. He answered latex and things that look like latex. Ok. I bought a little romper and texted him that day teasing him about the fun little outfit I had on. In his texts, the boy was sexually aggressive. Telling me he was hard and could not wait. He got to my apartment, came up the stairs and found me, casually lying on the bed with a silk robe and my latex dominatrix styled boots waiting for him to arrive. I was horny, all dressed up, and wanted him to react primally. I had told him previously that I like it when a guy is proactive, a bit aggressive, in the sex department. I had told him to kiss me, touch me, and if I did not want sex in that moment I would tell him. So there I was ready and waiting and expecting him to walk in and just rip that robe off of me like his texts had indicated. Instead he walks in, looks at me, gets on the bed, and…. just starts talking about the day. Twenty minutes later he gently starts touching the ties to the robe and timidly hints that maybe I should take it off. Undress myself. My vagina dried up and died. All those texts, me buying an outfit specifically for him, and teasing him about it, and he could not even act excited about it when he got into the bedroom. I was angry. Pissed. Felt stupid and ashamed. Embarrassed. When I tried to talk to him about it the next day, he avoided me. The only time he was able to talk about sex, was through text. In person he would shy away from it.

I broke it off because, I need sex. I need to talk to my boyfriend about sex. And toys. I want him to want to explore. I want him to walk in the room after a long day away and push me against the wall and kiss me to let me know how much he needs me. I really need a guy who will occasionally just push me against the wall when he kisses me. Like I really really need that in a relationship. That was definitely not him. He obviously needed someone with a bit less libido and a lot less kink. But that relationship was a good reminder to me that sex is pretty damn complicated. My sex personality is one thing, his was another, and they did not mesh well. And that is ok. But not everyone knows that or wants to accept this. There are people out there who think that if they truly love someone, the sex won't matter. They can get past their differences in bed. After all personality is most important right? Sex is an after thought. By the way, these differences and the inability to address them, that's why some people cheat. It isn't the only reason, but it's a reason.

I use the "Whisper" app. This confessions app lets you anonymously post a short confession or opinion. Almost every day there is someone posting about how they are better than others because they don't care about looks or sex in a relationship. They love their significant other's personality more than anything else and sex is just the icing on the cupcake. It isn't important. We need to stop obsessing about sex as a culture.

To that I say: sex, sex, and more sex. I am human. I have breasts that tingle, a neck that shivers from the touch of lips, oh and I have a vagina that gets wet and warm and tents to accommodate different-sized men. I was designed to have sex. So were you. So was everyone. Yes, I know that some people don't have high sex drives, or are asexual or, only react to emotional attraction. And I know that some people have medical conditions that make sex painful and impossible.I am not speaking about the exceptions to the rule or those medical conditions, I am speaking about the basic nature of humans to want to mate and procreate. The moment our hormones switch on, we want sex or some type of sexual contact. If a guy passes me on the street, I look at his biceps and his butt and his oh so fantastic hair. I can't help it. He looks at my boobs and butt and face. Only for a split second or it becomes disrespectful of course, but we all notice attractive people. We are designed to look for healthy counterparts. And even though we don't all want kids or to sleep with the opposite sex, we still crave some sort of sexual contact because of that biological imperative we are born with as animals.

It isn't the fact that we are sexual beings that causes all of our problems, it is our constant drive to deny it, ignore it, and act like we should be disgusted by it. Now I am not saying we have to become sex crazed lunatics who walk around jumping each other at every chance. I'm not saying that every time you see someone attractive on the street you should walk up to them and make inappropriate comments and try to force them in bed with you, that is a whole other problem that I am going to talk about later. I am saying that we need to be willing to acknowledge that sex is in our nature so we can open the conversation on how to have a healthy relationship with our bodies sexual needs and wants without overstepping our potential sexual partners' bodily autonomy, wants, needs, and without undermining their right to a healthy sexual relationship with their body. When we say that sex shouldn't matter. That it is just the icing or bonus to a relationship, we are closing the conversation. Making people feel like failures if they wake up one morning and realize they are so sexually frustrated that they want to cheat because in their relationship personality should matter more. When we don't talk about sex as if it is a normal, healthy part of life, we are casting it to the shadows. Making it seem like a taboo subject you shouldn't want to mention. Most religions and cultures would have you believe just that.

I have spoken a bit about how to start the sex conversation with kids. And I have spoken a bit on how teens have sex and need access to birth control and information. But now I want to focus, really really focus, for a while on what I started speaking about above. I want to focus for a bit on human nature because in reality, the conversation about sex must begin with the acknowledgment that we are sexual beings.

...Sex is Human Nature...

Did you know that cats have barbed penises? The sex isn't that great for the female cat. Spider females eat their mates after sex. That is how they are designed. Humans, we got lucky. We were designed to not just mate, but to enjoy the process. When I get wet, it doesn't just make sex easier, it makes it painless and fun. For the guy his foreskin helps add sensation, lubrication, and pleasure. The penile head has nerves upon nerves. My clit has more nerve endings than any other body part — male or female. Women are not just designed to have sex, we are designed to orgasm. Men don't just ejaculate, they release, they moan, they feel the ejaculation as a euphoric release. And women, we don't just lay there receiving, at least not when the sex is good, we feel it. We feel the friction and have moments sometimes continuously of pure pleasure when certain spots are touched and stroked and hit. We can have different types of orgasms from our clits, from inside of us, from both. It's why, despite not being spoken about openly, despite it being taboo in almost every culture, sexual pleasure is a bit of an obsession, especially for women.

If we are going to talk about how natural sex is, then we also have to talk about something else. I bleed. Every single month. Out of my vagina. For up to seven days. And the world around me, tells me that this is disgusting. Hide your tampons. Make sure no one notices when you take one out before you head to the restroom. If a tampon falls out of

your purse, pick it up as fast as humanely possible.
Oh and on the subject of normal things we have to
hide, guys get boners. It is normal. It happens. But
god forbid they wear the wrong pants and get a
random boner. If that happens we laugh or shame
them. Make fun of it. Even get them in trouble
because it happened at school. Pro tip: guys get
random boners and if you don't want to see it,
maybe move your eyes away from their crotch.
Don't run down the hall and try to get them kicked
out because you were accidentally exposed to a
noticeable bulge in his pants. Now if the boner is
outside of the pants and you are in public, that's not
ok and you can tell someone it made you
uncomfortable. If he rubs that bulge against you
without permission, tell someone. If someone

touches you without asking and you feel uncomfortable, tell someone. But don't look down, see a bulge, and immediately try to make a guy feel bad about it. If women could get hard ons, I would probably have one like sixty percent of most days. I wouldn't want to be made to feel ashamed of the fact that my arousal happened to be noticeable when yours is impossible to see.

But let's get back to periods. I bleed. But more than that, my hormones go insane. I cry more easily, crave chocolate, get irritated at the world, and want to curl up in bed with sweats, pizza, chocolate, and depending on the day, either a rom com or an action movie. Every girl is affected differently by their periods. Some are in so much pain they can't move. Some bleed so much they basically live in the bathroom. And some barely

notice it at all. But every single month fifty percent

of the world's population bleeds out of their vagina.

And we are made to feel dirty for it. We let you

stick your dick in there, not always knowing where

it has been, but god forbid we bleed. That's the

gross bit. But that isn't how it should work. You

don't get to say that the normal fluid that comes out

of my body is gross when you can talk about your

sperm and put your penis anywhere you want to

without anyone telling you, that your penis and

sperm are gross. If you mention your period, in

passing, because its part of your day, people

respond with *"too much information."* We can't talk

about tampons or pads because it is unseemly. We

have to go to our girlfriends and whisper, *"Do you*

have a tampon?" Because god forbid someone else hears that I am bleeding like I do every month and need something to prevent it from ruining my new Victoria Secret underwear. I used to be scared of telling the guy I was dating that I was having my period. I thought I had to hide it from him because how could he ever want to have sex with me if at some point blood came out of there? My first serious boyfriend freaked out when we had sex and my period started during it. I had no idea that could happen, but it did. He was wearing a condom but he looked down saw the blood then looked up at me, horrified.

"Did your period start?"

"I guess so. Sorry I didn't realize that it was starting soon."

"That so gross. I have to go take a shower.

How could you not realize that you were bleeding

on me?"

"I'm sorry. I'll come shower too."

"Not right now. I want to shower alone. And

you need to clean yourself."

That felt great. I mean really. That made me

feel so incredible. I felt no shame. I felt so wanted

and understood. Like my period was totally normal

and no big deal. We just needed to go shower clean

up and could laugh about this in a few minutes. By

the way, I use sarcasm to disguise my need to curl

up in a ball and cry for a month straight. Again, I let

you put your penis inside me, you don't get to judge

my period. My period has made me feel disgusting

at times. I have been having a period for about

twelve years now. If it lasted for five days each

month which it normally does, that's about seven

hundred and twenty days of bleeding, if you were to

add it all together. Of blood. Imagine feeling

disgusting and worthless and incapable of fixing

what made you feel that way for two years straight.

It isn't better because it's broken up with a few

weeks of non period between the period. Most girls

have these same feelings. Because we are taught to

hide it. And boys aren't taught how normal it really

is. We aren't just bleeding for the heck of it or

because we want to. Our underwear gets stained.

Do you really think we enjoy that? Get over it. Your

penis or fingers might suddenly have blood on them

because we didn't realize. Tampons are going to fall

out of our bags. But the reality is, one half of the

population is taught to hide ourselves for a week every month, and the other half, is never taught how to deal with the reality of what a period looks like.

The average age of menopause is fifty-one. If that's when I reach it, I will have had a period for forty years. In total that is two thousand and four hundred days of blood if I maintain a five day period each time. I'm not going to spend the rest of those one thousand six hundred and eighty days ashamed of that part of my life. And women, you shouldn't have to either. Reclaim your period because no one should spend nearly six and a half years of their lives total feeling gross and ashamed. And guys, once again, get over it. Blood is normal. We all have it. It won't kill you. Not in most circumstances at least. Every girl you have ever met has bled out of her vagina at some point or another. If you have sex with a girl chances are at some point she is gonna bleed on you. Tampons don't bite. Just deal with it and help us live in a world where we feel safe to admit that we are bleeding and might be slightly emotional because of it.

Also, small announcement, even when not having our period, it is normal for our vagina's to discharge fluids. Unless it smells really weird or has a very unnatural color, that fluid means your va jay jay is working properly and cleaning itself. Guys, penises can have discharges too. Normally with hard ons, if it's happening a lot and you have other uncomfortable symptoms, go see a doctor. This goes for both genders.

So let's review. Hard ons are normal, periods are normal, and sex is normal. Human bodies are incredible are they not?

But somehow we have ended up in this place where we feel the need to deny this in polite company. With friends, of course we talk shop. But you don't go around talking about sex or the human body with anyone else. We talk about medical problems, sports, education, and so many other things that happen normally in our lives, but we don't talk about sex. It is hidden away like the black market. Now I am not an expert, but obviously something happened. So on that note, I want to mention religion.

...Teaching Only Abstinence...

Disclaimer: I am not an expert on history or religion. I am in no way an expert on the evolution of human sexuality and religion. This section is based only on my experiences and my opinions and I would love to hear what you think too.

My mom was raised Irish Catholic. My father was raised French Catholic. The basic teachings for Catholicism say that you should not have sex before marriage. Masturbation is a sin. And depending on how you interpret it, homosexuality is unnatural and should be condemned. Also birth control is a no no. Sex is for babies and married people using birth control are interfering with God. Not that there was ever weird sex in the Bible. Lot and his daughters in a cave. Lot giving his daughters up to be raped by the men at his door. But no nothing weird about sex in the Bible.

My mom and dad have told me about their families because they wanted me to understand where they came from. Neither of them had it easy. My mom's parents were big believers in their faith. Which is how my mom ended up in a family of six, despite the family not being able to afford the many mouths to feed and bodies to clothe. My mom and her siblings were shown very varied levels of affection and its pretty clear that that has lead to some disfunction even within the siblings themselves. And maybe that is more of a failure on her parents' ability to parent than anything else, but

I can't help but wonder if the differences would have been so obvious with less kids. Maybe the varied affections came from the frustration of not having enough to go around when suddenly there were six. All I know is, my grandparents, being married humans had a sex life and did not believe in preventing any sexual exploit from possibly ending in a baby. And while babies may seem cute and like a blessing at first, you have to raise them. They need food, education, toys, and clothing. The sad fact is, not everyone who wants a baby can afford the baby. And if you have it anyway, it's the baby that is going to suffer without a choice in the matter.

So you end up with six kids who may not have a chance to afford higher education. My mom had to work as a chambermaid in cheap motels, and at one point had to drop out of her dream school because of a lack of money. I'm not saying that people with less kids can't end up in that situation, but in my mom's case, the correlation is pretty clear. With six kids requiring constant around the clock funds, how do you ever save up enough to help them later on? You can't. Unless you make a lot of money and let's face it, we can't all be well off.

Part of me has always been angry about my mom's past. When I was old enough to really understand the cause and effect of things, I got angry at my grandparents. I wanted to scream at them. *"How dare you not use even a condom? If you can't afford that many kids and don't want to stop having sex, then wake up and take responsibility for your actions and desires. Don't*

want to stop having sex, use birth control. Don't

want to use birth control, then make sure you can

provide for the hundred kids you might create." Part

of the problem, of course, was that my grandfather

was an alcoholic and couldn't always keep a job.

But that didn't stop my grandparents from popping

out six kids. I'm not saying my mom's childhood

was completely horrible so please don't assume

that. My mom has good memories too. But if I am

going to speak about my realities around sex, I have

to talk about my parents' and grandparents' sex

lives too. Because they are a part of my history.

My dad's parents had a dysfunctional

relationship too, though it wasn't as based in

religion. My dad's dad was also an alcoholic and

was not present in my dad's life because, as he

reminded my father a lot, my dad was a mistake. An accident. By the way, I think if my dad was an accident, then he's the best accident ever. Because I got a father who was incredibly honest with me about his mistakes and his parents' mistakes. He understood that admitting to me that his family and he weren't perfect, so it was normal and ok for me to mess up too, would be healthy for me in the long run. And he was right. I have messed up a lot. But hearing that my dad did too, helped me understand the importance of failure in development and growing up. My grandmother on my dad's side was not a very comforting or affectionate parent either. She was far more caring towards my father then towards my aunt. My grandmother was a big believer in the fact that men were more important because they carried the family name. She used to say that my dad was the baby Jesus. My aunt never had an affectionate nickname. This carried through to my grandmother's treatment of my brother and me. My baby brother was the son of Jesus, me, well I was the whore who wore nail polish on my thirteenth birthday. I mean she loved me too, but there was definitely more criticism towards me, my aunt, and my female cousins then there was towards my father and brother. That is not to say that my grandmother was good to my dad. Neither of my parents were treated amazingly well by their parents.

But let's get back to religion. My mom admitted to me early on that even though her parents were strong believers in abstinence until marriage and no birth control, she did not follow the same thought process. My mom came right out and told me she had not waited until marriage. She and my dad slept together without ever letting my grandparents know. They were not even allowed to stay in the same room until they were married when visiting the in laws. But this didn't stop them from having a sex life. My mom told this to me to reassure me that sex was normal in relationships. She even told me at one point that if I got to age twenty-two and had not had sex, it would be ok to find a nice boy and just do it. After all, my body has needs and denying them is not healthy. But Catholicism, and most religions in fact, would have you believe that those natural urges and temptations are a test. Submitting to them, a failure. They would also have you believe that sex is not complicated. When you get married, sex will just start on your wedding night. There is no mention of the possibility of different libidos, different sexual wants and desires, different needs, or even the possibility that his penis might be too big or too small for it to ever feel good. Instead most religions assume that because you are in love, everything will just work out perfectly. And if it doesn't, it doesn't really matter because if you follow the most strict version of most religions, then as a wife it is your duty to tend to your husband's needs. Your needs and comfort be damned. The arranged marriages in many cultures ignore these facts and possibilities too.

Sexual compatibility cannot be forced. Sure sometimes you meet someone who you don't really think of sexually but after weeks of talking and close intimate conversation you begin to realize you are also physically attracted to them. And sure that situation can work out perfectly. But the truth of the matter is that we are not all sexually compatible with one another. The idea that just because you are married or in love, the sex will work is naive and oversimplified. Now, of course, I have many other problems with arranged marriages. The idea that women are property to be traded for different things. The concept that a woman has no choice in part of her life. That her body is not actually considered to be hers. The fact that in many of these cultures the girls are minors as young as ten if not younger. And I do understand that there are some woman who want these arranged marriages, I don't judge any one if that is your choice, it is when it was not your choice but you parents', families', and cultures' choice that the my problems start. In many of these arranged marriages, it is not about the girl's choice, it is about a power, status, or financial shift for the family. These girls are then forced to have sexual relationships with men they never chose to have in their lives. When these girls go along with it because of their fear or commitment to their family, or even because they have been taught that it is not their choice since they were little, this is a type of rape. These girls never even have a chance to experience the body autonomy that we all, as human beings, should have the right to.

I do recognize of course that this can happen to men too but as I can only speak from the female perspective, I would rather let a guy talk about the male perspective on this matter. My reason for this, is very specific. Women and men play very different roles in sex. Again, I am not speaking to the sex between gay individuals, transgendered individuals, or anything beyond the man and woman sex relationship since this is the one I have experience with. But when I have sex with a man, no matter what the situation, there is a type of submission that I as a female go through. Not in a negative way, just when looking at basic anatomy. I was designed to have a foreign body inside me. He was designed to put himself in a foreign body. Because of this, when my body is not committed to the sex, it can hurt. Of course men can have painful experiences sexually, but in a general sex situation, when things go wrong I am at more risk in a very basic way. Both of us can get STDs, but I can get pregnant. He can go flaccid, but if we are having sex and I am not ready or I lose my arousal, the simple act of him trying to continue the sex is going to become very painful for me. My vagina was not designed to have sex without lubrication. So, when I am not attracted to someone or when I do not want sex with someone, if the sex were to happen anyway it would be very painful for me.

I cannot imagine that the girls in those arranged marriages are always aroused or prepared by their husbands before penetrative sex. Are they even told what sex looks like before their new husbands start stripping their clothes of off? If I am wrong, then obviously it is because no one speaks openly and honestly about how sex in arranged marriages is approached. And of course there are arranged marriages that are not forced and maybe because of that it is less awkward or problematic. Like I said before I am no expert in other religions or the history of human sexuality. I am speaking right now as a white female in America who has heard stories and knows how my body functions during sex. If I am not aroused enough, I can't even masturbate with my dildos because it hurts to try and put something inside.. But I do know that many cultures and many religions around the world teach only abstinence before marriage. I really believe that even in cultures and religions where this is taught, sex should still at least be discussed. It does not have to be encouraged. But at least talk about erections and lubrication and how the anatomy is supposed to work when boy and girl get down to business. At the very least this would help women and men approach their wedding night with the knowledge needed to help make sex less awkward. Maybe then if the sex did not work or feel great at first, the couple would know how to comfortably discuss the possible reasons and solutions. Maybe then they could at least not feel like failures because the sex wasn't miraculously perfect because rings were exchanged and both had kept to their vow of innocence until that night.

You see, I understand that my perspective belongs only to me. People should be allowed to wait until marriage because they want to. Have an arranged marriage if it is truly one hundred percent their decision. But I also believe that we need to recognize sex as a normal activity and start actually talking about it so that when we are ready to get naked, we can approach it safely, with enthusiasm, and with the tools necessary to adapt if something goes wrong.

Abstinence only education, ignores the fact that sex will occur eventually. It ignores the possibility that you may slip up and have sex before marriage, because humans make mistakes. Abstinence only, is the result of adults believing that they have or should have total control over their children and ignoring the possibility that kids don't always listen to their parents. Think of how many teenagers get pregnant each year. Sure some of them just decided not to use a condom because teens are immature and do not have fully developed brains, but many teens just don't know enough about sex to understand how easily pregnancy occurs. Many teens are too scared to ask their parents or adults for birth control or condoms but because they are teenager, they are still going to have sex. Abstinence only education leads to an environment where parents won't talk sex and kids become too scared to ask their parents about it. We only know how to talk and walk because we watch our parents. They teach us right from wrong and how to maneuver in this world. If your parents never brought up sex or only did to tell you not to do it, would you feel comfortable going to them because at sixteen you really wanted to sleep with your significant other? Or would you instead feel so uncomfortable that you never mentioned your relationship to them and would rather risk pregnancy and STDs than face their wrath at discovering you were a sexual being?

If we look at abstinence only education, we must also return to the fact that teenagers are rebellious, horny, and stubborn people. I mentioned the screaming matches I had with my mom remember? Almost every teen has some type of rebellious streak to them. And when you throw in those hormones, is it any wonder that it's a stereotype in every high school movie that the teens are making out everywhere? Behind the bleachers, in mom's car. I mean really the amount of relationships in high school no matter how short or long is a pretty good indication that teens feel the hormones. So when you take a rebellious horny fifteen year old and tell them not to have sex, do you really think they are going to listen?

Something like sixteen million girls between fifteen and nineteen give birth around the world each year. That is a lot of teen sex, especially when you realize that number is only about the girls who got pregnant, not the number of teens actually doing the deed. Continuing with this train of thought, a survey conducted a few years ago found that around seventy percent of all teenagers thought that they should have access to birth control in case they start having sex. Abstinence only education, ignores these statistics, ignores reality, and looks at the world through rose colored glasses. If we tell teens not to until marriage, they won't. If they do, then they have failed in the eyes of God or the family. Teens that come from abstinence only backgrounds are made to feel shame and are often disowned or punished if it is found that they have had sex. Many of these kids, if they end up pregnant, get kicked out of the house. The problem with this is that these kids are punished for something that could have been avoided had they had access to birth control and a sexual education based on their reality instead of the reality of their parents.

You might be religious. You may have waited until marriage to have sex. But that in no way means your kid is obligated to do the same. You can want them to. You can try to teach them to.

But at the end of the day it is their life and their decision. You can teach abstinence, as long as you realize that it might not be what your kid wants and you prepare them and yourself for that reality. Tell them that it is what you did and that you would love for them to do the same, but then still teach them about sex and birth control and how to handle problems that may arise. Don't teach your kid to fear needing you when this type of problem arises. Don't teach them that they are failures if they do not follow in your footsteps. That is not healthy, it is cruel. We all turn eighteen eventually and are expected to live on our own as adults; and that is only possible if we learn to make choices for ourselves as we grow up. Treating your kid like your property until the magical eighteenth birthday harms your child more than it helps. This is especially true with sex as it can lead to disease, pregnancy, and then responsibility for another human life.

...Birth Control and Abortion...

These Are Not New Concepts, And it is My body, My Choice

The above leads us to another important conversation. Every time I have sex, I risk getting pregnant. My body is always at risk. But this is true for every single women who is sexually active. Even women who are told they are infertile have miraculously become pregnant. This is problematic because in this day and age, not everything is about procreation. We live in an overpopulated world where we are each expected to grow up, get jobs, and be independent. Even before this was the case, women have always recognized that pregnancy is a possibility and attempted to have control over this.

In cultures around the world women have put things inside their vaginas to prevent pregnancy. Honey, lint, and crocodile dung are just three examples of things women would put inside themselves as a birth control method. They would eat different plants, breast feed for three years, and even ingest oil and gold in attempts to prevent pregnancy. Men would try to prevent ejaculation inside of the women. Abortion too is found in ancient cultures around the world. Since women realized that certain activities or foods could force miscarriages, women have aborted fetuses. Women would even resort to letting themselves be beaten or wearing extremely tight girdles to terminate pregnancies. The reason for all of this is very, very simple. Women, though capable of being pregnant, are not and have never considered themselves to only be incubators.

Bodily autonomy is very simply, the fact that we each have control over our own body. We cannot be forced to donate blood, organs, or tissue. Even when we are dead, we still maintain our right to our body. It is why we have to have donor on our licenses if we want to give our organs when we pass. My body belongs to me and me alone. My parents may have given birth to me, but they do not have the right to make decisions about my body for me. Of course as minors, our parents have certain rights over us, but that is done because we cannot make legal decisions before we turn eighteen. But even our parents don't have complete rights over us. Patient doctor confidentiality for many things is still in place for minors. My doctor could not tell my parents if I was pregnant without my permission, for example.

This body autonomy means that I make decisions about my body. If I want to have sex, I have the right to have sex. Of course my partner also has the right to decide if he wants sex or not too. When both of us individually decide that we want sex together, we have sex. If one of us decided to have sex with the other, and did not get permission, that is rape and is illegal because someone has invaded our right to our own body. I have the right to want sex, without immediately wanting a baby. Not everyone wants a baby. I don't. I have zero maternal instincts and have had so many medical problems throughout my life that I do not ever want to be pregnant and add extra risks to my life. And pregnancy does carry a lot of risks. Women die from childbirth in every culture, religion, and environment. Even in first world hospitals women die in childbirth. Because it is a medical condition.

There are people who would tell me and have told me, *"Well, if you don't want a baby then don't have sex."* That is unfair. That is telling me that I should ignore all of my sexual feelings because I don't want a baby. And it is unfair because men don't have that same danger. Sure when a baby is born the guy can be on the hook financially, but they do not carry the baby. They do not have the medical risks. Now I am a strong advocate that if a guy and girl have sex and get pregnant, if the man does not want a baby and expresses this to the woman, I do not think he should be forced to care for a baby he does not want. This is especially true if the couple was using birth control. But in the same manner, I do not think a woman should be forced to carry a baby she does not want. We should not lose our body autonomy just because we had sex and the birth control failed. You cannot pick and choose body autonomy. You cannot tell me that I can't be forced to donate blood but I can be forced to share my body with another life form. Until the fetus in my uterus is capable of thriving outside of my body, it is not a life or a baby, it is a parasite. It is stealing nutrients from me, taking up space in my body, and putting my life at risk.

I am also told that if I am that worried about getting pregnant and that unwilling to remain abstinent, I should just get my tubes tied. That is funny. I actually have tried to find places that would tie my tubes. But I don't have three kids, and I am not over twenty-five or thirty, the age depends on the state, so I am not legally allowed to get my tubes tied. Because what if I change my mind? I have a biological clock after all. I have a uterus. Obviously I have to want babies eventually. Actually, no, hold on just one moment.

I do not want a baby. I do not hear a clock. If I did change my mind, then there are other ways to get babies. Adoption for example. If I make a decision and regret it, so what, we all regret decisions we make. But for some reason I am just not actually allowed to make that decision for myself because of the small chance that I might just happen to change my mind. Why aren't men told the same thing? They get vasectomies left and right. At age eighteen. Nobody questions a guy when he says that he doesn't want kids. And vasectomies are not always reversible. If he regrets his vasectomy he would have to consider adoption. But he can still get his tubes tied. Sometime I really do hate my uterus. It is used against me a lot in these situations. I have the right to have sex, be on birth control, and legally get an abortion, but god forbid I want a permanent birth control solution before I have the baby I seriously do not want. But then again, I am a woman, I should not be having enough sex to need my tubes tied. Right? But let's return to the original topic of this section. Abortion.

Of course the abortion conversation becomes very complicated when we look at surrogacy or when the fetus could survive on its own. But that is why we need to have more conversations. There was a case in the news recently where a surrogate ended up pregnant with three fetuses. Most of the time only one embryo implants which is why multiple are placed inside of a surrogate or a women using IVF. It is to increase the chances of one taking. But in this case three did. Now with multiples, reducing the number of embryos gives the remaining ones a better chance of developing fully. The couple who's fetuses they are, wants to reduce the pregnancy to two, but the surrogate who is actually pregnant does not want to go through an abortion. Here there is no right answer. Of course this possibility is one that should become a conversation beforehand for all those who go through implantation whether it is their body or another's. The babies belong to one couple, but are in the body of another person. So who has more right to the medical decisions. In this situation it is extremely complicated, but in mine it should be very simple.

I don't want a baby. My body has to carry the baby and every risk that goes with it. I get to decide if I want to stay pregnant. And yes I understand why men get angry about this, I really do. I know it takes two to tango and the fetus has half my genetic material and half yours, but this is why we need to have a conversation before we have

sex. I am on birth control, but in the event that it

fails and I were to get pregnant, I will abort. No

matter what. If a guy has a problem with that, I will

not sleep with him or will stop sleeping with him. If

you don't believe in abortion, don't sleep with

someone who does, and if you do, then don't be

upset when you realize that a pregnancy has

happened and they are sticking to what they said

they would do. There are girls and guys out there

who don't believe in abortion and those who do, no

one is forcing you to sleep with someone that

believes different then you do on this subject and if

they are, then that's an entirely different problem

and conversation. But at the end of the day there is

only one thing that matters when it comes to birth

control and abortion. It is my body and I choose what happens to it. It is that simple. If you don't approve of abortion, don't have one but don't force your decisions on me.

I want to reiterate, I understand why guys get angry when a woman wants to abort the fetus created by the two of them. But biology is unfair. Men can ot get pregnant. They are not the ones with the medical risks, the ones who have to go through labor, and the ones who have to breastfeed for up to a year afterwards. They don't deal with the hormones. I mean sure if they stay with the girl while she is pregnant they see the hormones and are subjected to the women's' emotional rollercoaster, but guys, that girl is the one who's body and mind is changing in ways she has no control over. We are the ones who can get postpartum depression. Women sometimes kill their own babies because of those hormones. That is how fucked up we get. We are the ones who can't leave the situation for even one second. You can go to work or to the store or drink to have a break. We can't leave the pregnancy. Not for one second during those nine months. So yes biology is unfair and that fetus has some of your genetic material, but it isn't fair to us either that you don't have the option of being pregnant and cannot take that burden from us. I am the one who bleeds every month and relies on that blood to tell me whether I am pregnant or not. I am the one who has to pay attention to my body constantly in case I get pregnant. So I have to be the one who ultimately decides whether I want to spend nine months catering to another being that I will not get a moment's break from. It is unfair but so is the fact that I am the one at risk of all of this happening to me.

So abortion has to be my choice, but there is a way we could prevent abortion from being as prevalent as it is. There is such a thing as birth control. Condoms protect against STDS and pregnancy, but condoms do break and some people are allergic to them. Luckily, there are different types of birth control available for women. Unluckily, they are very expensive and not always easy to have access to. In college I started on Loestrin Fe. Its one of the more mild beginner birth control pills. I was nauseous for the first month of taking them, had to take them around the same time every day, and had to get the prescription refilled every few months. Over the summer, my school insurance cut out and I learned that without it, my pills were seventy dollars. A month. If I couldn't afford insurance, I would be paying over eight hundred dollars a year that as a college student, I could not have afforded. There are thousands of women around the world who cannot afford birth control, and while condoms are great for these women, they aren't perfect. They break. Which is why abortion is so important. These women can't even afford birth control yet we expect them to be a able to afford a pregnancy, a child. Even the abortion costs quite a bit because of all the legality involved. And not every place offers abortion. So we need more access to affordable birth control. But instead of recognizing this, the world around us tries to twist the situation back on us.

"Just don't have sex if you don't want a baby."

"Birth control is not a right."

"This company is religious. We don't believe in birth control so we won't cover it for our employees."

"We are not going to pay for you to go around having sex."

"If you can't afford a baby, then get on birth control."

"You can't murder that baby. You should have either gone on birth control or kept your legs closed."

Read all those statements again. Can you see

how twisted and confusing and frustrating this is for

us of the uteri.? There is no easy answer. And do not

say abstinence. I am twenty-three years old and

have needs and the right to have sex. It is not fair

that men can go around having sex without these

same worries. Sure they can get STDs and if a

woman gets pregnant they are expected to stick

around and help, but it really is not the same. And if

you cannot see that, then go take a survey with both

men and women and the way they feel about sex

and pregnancy. I guarantee to you women fear

pregnancy more. I guarantee you that women are

more frustrated about birth control access and cost.

And I guarantee you that women are told more

often then men to keep their legs closed if they don't

want a baby. The conversation has always been stacked against women. It is why feminism exists and will always exist in some way. We don't want women to have more power, we want the same amount that men have and have always had. We want our sex lives to be as acknowledged and considered the same as men's. And we want to have non baby creating sex with the same ease as our male counterparts. But we won't be able to until we can get birth control more easily.

There is this conversation going around right now. This new birth control called Vasalgel is being tested. It is injected into the male anatomy and prevents sperm from traveling through the penis and into the vagina for ten years. Its also easily reversible. People are talking about the possible costs and the possible ease with which it will be accessible. The running joke is that it will be very cheap and very easy to get. Even if this turns out not to be true, you have to ask why we think this will be the case.?Why are we so quick to assume that male birth control will be so easy to get when female birth control is so difficult? The answer is simple. When it comes to sex, the way men and woman talk about it and are told to act about it, is inherently different.

…The Battle of the Sexes…

I was born a girl. With breasts, a vagina, and all the stereotypes that go along with my inherent and obvious femininity. Starting from childhood it was obvious to me the way I was treated was different then the way my brother or other boys were treated. My parents, luckily tried as hard as possible not to make me feel different then my brother when it came to clothes, activities, and what I was capable of. They encouraged me to explore sports, science, and subjects like wood shop. But I was not always around my parents. In the outside world, it was very obvious to me that my gender, and therefore I, was considered weaker and less intelligent then the guys around me. It seems subtle at first, you realize that the way toys are designed is based on the idea that girls want pretty and pink and guys want action and strength. The television shows reflect this too. Then as you get older you hear the jokes.

"You throw like a girl."

"Grow a pair."

"Don't be a pussy."

The jokes and sayings all imply one thing. Girls are weaker then boys. Girls should be feminine and dainty. Guys should be tough and masculine. It hurts both genders. Boys who like the color pink and want to ride horses are made fun of and girls who want to learn martial arts and cut their hair short are told they are not girly enough. But as you get older those subtle differences begin to show in a new way. When puberty hits, girls are exposed to a new reality. We become sex objects in a much more obvious and harmful way then our male counterparts. Every advertisement uses both genders to sell but women are generally more naked. In video games and television shows about the female heroes, girls are always exposed. We are told that now that our breasts have come in, we have to be more careful. Wear bras and don't wear low cut tops because men will get the wrong idea, as if men are so hardwired to stare that they are literally incapable of controlling themselves around a pair of breasts. You have to shave because men will think you are gross if you don't. Wax your bikini area or no man will want to go down on you.

We also learn a new very terrifying truth. We cannot and should never walk alone.

It starts the moment you have visible breasts. You are walking down the street and a guy walks up to you and tells you that you are beautiful. The first time it happens, it is kind of sweet. You realize that the opposite sex is attracted to you. But you don't respond readily because you aren't supposed to talk to strangers and you are sixteen, maybe younger, and not sure what to think. But then you realize that this is not a rare occurrence. It happens every day when you are alone and sometimes with other girls. And then he tells you, you are beautiful and out of politeness you say thanks while trying to walk away, and he follows you. Maybe just for a moment, maybe for a whole block. Or he tells you, you should smile and you

can't help but wonder why it is his business, why he

felt compelled to say it. I have never just walked up

to someone to say something to them without

provocation. Then he isn't just telling you, you are

pretty, he gets angry when you try to continue on

your day. So you start to fear the street. You start

hearing about the girl who told someone to leave

her alone and was murdered. You hear about the

rape that happened in the alley that you walk by

every day. And you start to see the other side of

becoming a developed girl. You start to feel like you

should never walk by yourself. Like you should

always have a guy friend with you. You go buy a

taser or pepper spray. Watch self defense videos.

The first time your car breaks down you realize you

are terrified of getting out and asking for help. What if the guy who stops to help kidnaps you or helps and then forces you to sleep with him in return. You realize that on every first date you want to tell your best friend that if you haven't texted at a certain time she should call the police. You drive yourself and fear even letting him walk you to your car in the dark parking lot behind the restaurant. When you sell or buy something off of Craigslist you make sure you are never alone. Men don't have these thoughts. They may fear getting mugged, but most men, if you ask them for an honest answer, will tell you they are not afraid of walking down the street. Most girls are.

Last year I locked myself out of my running car in a McDonalds parking lot. It was sunny and around noon in a very busy area and the McDonalds had a video camera pointing directly at my car. I was in my work clothes jeans and a long sleeve shirt. It was not revealing at all. But as I was waiting for the mechanic, I never felt safe. Within the first five minutes of this experience a man around twenty-seven had slowed his car down and started yelling at me to get my attention. He wasn't asking if I needed help. He was just yelling, *"Hey Chica you look fine."* He kept yelling it until the light in front of him turned green and he drove off. He didn't stop after I acknowledged him by making eye contact. Another man was waiting on the other side of the street, noticed me and started yelling as he crossed, *"Hey. Hey. Hey. You should smile girl. Hey girl. Hey."* I was afraid as he approached the side of the street I was on that I would have to run into the McDonalds just to avoid him. Again this is in daylight. In a busy area. In the half hour I waited, four men yelled at me. Four men thought that because I was there, they should yell at me. Force me to acknowledge their existence and thank them for the attention. But it did not feel good. I was minding my own business in an already stressful situation and instead of it feeling like I was being complimented, it felt like my existence belonged to them. Freedom of speech doesn't mean the freedom to harass me. It doesn't mean that just because I am standing there, you should force your presence onto me.

At the bar when I am out with friends, if you come up to me and after an exchange I excuse myself, I am not interested. But that does not seem to matter. Men have gotten angry when I wanted to walk back to my friends. As if the fact that they were interested in me meant I had to give them my attention. I have heard other girls tell me that they have been followed around the bar almost into bathrooms. Sometimes into the bathrooms. On the dance floor if we move away from your dancing, it doesn't seem to matter to you. If you buy me a drink, you did that of your own volition, you cannot be angry that I won't give you any attention. If I do happen to give you attention, I have the right at any time to decide I want to leave, so do you. So why am I the one who feels threatened? You seem to be under the impression that you can choose what girl you want next to you, but I should be honored when you choose me and I should just accept it and be grateful.

Fathers, boyfriends, husbands, men, this is the world we live in. You cannot tell us to just leave if we are not interested because we all have examples of when leaving turned violent for us or another girl. We cannot be forward for the same reason. We stand there uncomfortably making small chat trying to figure out if you are one of the nice and respectful ones, or if you are going to be the one that makes us a statistic. And the sad thing is, if we misstep and become that statistic, we are the ones who get blamed. Because we were drinking, or wearing the short skirt, or we didn't leave the conversation the moment we felt uncomfortable. We are prudes if we don't give you the time of day, but we are whores if we do too quickly. We are no fun if we leave because we don't feel comfortable, but if we stay and something goes wrong it is our fault for not leaving soon enough. We can't win.

I told my brother this summer after an uncomfortable walk downtown. Middle of the day in New Haven, Conneticut. I had gone shopping and had to walk through the town green. This is a college town, it is busy, and it was the middle of the day. In that half an hour walk, I was hit on ten times. I was told to smile, that I was sexy, damn I had fine legs, my ass was fine, I should smile because I would be prettier. None of it made me feel good. In half an hour I went from Olivia who just wanted to go shopping by myself to a piece of meat that belonged to every man who took one glance. It made me feel like the street belonged to them, not

me. I did not have the right to walk in peace and go

about my day. No, I was there to be looked at,

commented on, and examined like a museum or zoo

exhibit. Ask any girl in your life, she has felt the

same way. But the worst of this was, when I told my

brother, he told me I was overreacting. That they

were just compliments. I should not feel threatened

by it. No woman has ever denied the fear felt by

other women when we walk down the street. Only

guys do. Guys always do. Which is funny since they

are not the ones experiencing this every day.

When I tell you I was scared, you do not get

to tell me that I am overreacting. You were not

there. You don't see the expression in their eyes like

I am a piece of meat. You don't feel them follow

you for five paces, ten, a whole block. You have

never felt compelled to run into the nearest shop

and just want to collapse into tears because you hate

your own body because it is the reason you felt so

scared and you just needed to get off the street and

away from the leers and words that have followed

you for the last ten years. No. You do not get to tell

me that I am overreacting. The entire female

population is not overreacting. If half the world is

telling you that we feel a certain way, it is time to

acknowledge that maybe you don't know better than

us. Maybe you should take our word for it and help

us find a way to make the world feel safer. I want to

walk outside in New Haven in the middle of the day

without feeling like I am on red alert for my life,

safety, and body. I fear rape more than I fear death. That is my truth. Because I am a girl.

The internet and internet dating is not an escape from this either. When I try the internet dating thing for every one comment that is nice and a decent conversation starter, there are twenty to a hundred comments just on my boobs. Or my ass. Or on how I should go to his place and suck his cock.. When I say no, I am a bitch, a prude, ugly... it goes on and on and on. It sort of makes you hate men after a while. It makes you want to just give up and never even risk leaving your house or going online ever again. Ask a girl in your life. She will tell you it has happened to her too. And yes, girls can be inappropriate creeps too, I am in no way denying that, but when you look at a general picture of the world and the way the two sexes are treated. You are a strong stand alone man who deserves power, sex, the paycheck; and I am the walking fleshlight there for your entertainment that should be thankful for the attention and whatever small consideration I do get in the workforce. I should be happy I even get that.

Still think that women are treated equally and I am overreacting? Go on youtube and find interviews with celebrities. The majority ask the men about their acting or lives while the women are asked about their dresses, how they lost the weight, or how they feel being a girl in that role surrounded by those men.

The main point I am trying to make is that when you grow up a girl, you grow up being constantly reminded that you do not have the same

rights as the men your age, you don't live in the

same world. I should wear make up because it is

what girls do, but to much make up is lying and I

should be happy with my natural looks. I have to

shave or men will find me disgusting and I won't

ever have a real boyfriend. My breasts are there to

feed babies when I have them, but until then they

are about sex. I cannot walk around half naked

because they are sexual. And if I could, I wouldn't

want to because of the way guys act when they see

boobies. If I do have a baby, I still have to keep the

nipple covered even when that baby is feeding,

because kids might see a sexual trait. Because men

cannot be expected to handle themselves around

breasts. Because breasts are so very very different

then a man's chest. I mean my nipples are just so so different from a man's nipples. It doesn't really make sense but then again guys act very creepy about breasts when I am wearing shirts so I am not even sure I want to walk around half naked. If I wear a short skirt I am doing it for attention and I am being trashy, but if I wear pants everyday I am unfeminine. When I say I don't walk alone out of fear, I am told I should not judge a whole gender like that, but every time I try to walk alone I am reminded of why that fear exists. If I don't have sex I am a prude, but too much sex or an openness towards sex and I am a used up whore that no man would want to touch. If I don't want to try new things in bed, I am no fun, but if I want to try too many, I must be some type of kinky slutty freak. I have not gone one day of my life since puberty

without being reminded of this reality at least once.

Part of the problem is that whether due to religion,

culture, or just plain ignorance, women are spoken

about in very degrading manners when sex is the

subject.

"If she has had sex too often, she is

probably loose down there which is no fun."

"She is all used up, I don't want to stick it

where other men have. I don't like leftovers."

There is this word that's been going around

for a while that demonstrates pretty heavily the

degradation shown towards women who enjoy sex.

Urban dictionary has several definitions for this

word.

"Any girl who takes loads of semen inside her,"

"a person who is addicted to being ejaculated in. Also see whore or slut,"

"a female receptacle for many men," and

" a receptacle for you and the rest of your town to put your semen in. Said receptacle is usually a slutty ho."

The word described here, is cum dumpster. And it is used a lot online. And it almost always refers to a female. Men speak often about masturbation and sex. In every television show, bar, online forum, and many every day situations, guys are just being guys when they talk about their latest conquest. But the girl they slept with, because she was easy or willing to go home with him after one

drink, she was slutty. He is just a guy, I am the used
up whore. Even if that isn't the intention, that's what
we girls hear. It's how we are treated. And it hurts.
And it makes us scared of exploring our selves and
our sexuality. I love sex, I really do, but I cannot tell
you how often after a masturbation session or a
sexual encounter I have moments where I feel
ashamed. What would my family and friends think?
Should I be honest in relationships or will he dump
me because my number is not one or two? If I
make the first move will he see me as bossy, too
forward, too aggressive, or will he be one of the few
that finds it endearing and proof of my self
confidence? This truth and reality that most of us
girls face, becomes even more apparent and

dangerous when we finally look at consent and

boundaries in these sexual relationships.

...Am I allowed to Say No...

I decided to write all of this down for
several reasons. First, it was cathartic for me to
replay that morning, write it down, and take an
honest look around me. But the real reason I
decided to write this is, I was and am angry.

I am angry that in twenty-sixteen, with all
the science and technological and cultural
advancements that our world has made, we cannot
even have real, open conversations about sex,
consent, boundaries, birth control, abortion, and
every other possible thing that comes up when you
think sex.

I am angry that when someone I trusted took
advantage of a situation it was not taken seriously

because of the lack of violence and because of the specific circumstances involved.

I am angry that girls around the world are mutilated so they cannot feel sexual pleasure.

Angry that girls in some cultures can be forced to marry and then have sex as early as nine years old.

Angry that when a nine year old is raped by her father, she can be forced to continue a life risking pregnancy at nine fucking years old without choice.

Angry that when population control is in place, it is the female babies that are killed or left on the side of the road to die. Because girls are less valuable then men.

I am angry that I cannot walk down the street without some guy commenting on my body and making me feel unsafe in my own body.

Angry that every decision I make about my body, my clothes, and what I do with my vagina is a double edged sword.

I am angry. And sad. And confused. And I am scared.

Scared of the fact that there are so many other girls out there who are going to go through what I went through, or worse, with no ability to turn to the people around them and ask for help.

Scared for the girls who think that because they were violated, and girls can be used up, no one will ever want to touch them again.

And I am scared for the girls like me, who despite having all the tools, despite having the right conversations, despite owning their sexuality, still end up being taken advantage of because we did not know how to talk about our boundaries. Did not know that we had to preemptively say no to every possible situation we didn't want to experience.

I am going to talk now about consent. I have mentioned it a few times, but now I want to dive deeply into the very simple, yet somehow very complicated world of consent. So let's break this down.

You and I hit it off. We find ourselves somewhere private and are kissing passionately. We both start removing each others clothing, one of us mentions condoms, the other nods, and a few moments later you are inside me. At what point in this scenario does either of us lose our right to leave the situation? The right answer, we don't. We never lose our right to say stop. To say no.

If I agree to sleep with you when you are wearing a condom, and you remove it at any point without asking me, the sex becomes nonconsensual.

If I tell you I am on birth control, when I am not, the sex is nonconsensual.

If we lie to each other about STDS, nonconsensual.

If we get back to your place, get naked, you are hard, and I decide I do not want to continue, it may suck for you, but I am allowed to leave.

If you are the one who wants to leave, you are allowed to leave no matter what happened before.

If either of us makes threats to coerce the other into having sex with us, the sex is nonconsensual.

If we are getting busy and I try to leave and you push me down, anything after that is nonconsensual.

If you are hard but unconscious and I get on top of you, that is nonconsensual.

If I am wet and asleep and you penetrate me in any way, that is nonconsensual.

Is this starting to make sense yet? The examples above seem simple, black and white, but not every situation is so simple. Even the above examples are debated constantly. The solution

seems so simple, ask. Make sure you get a yes. It

may seem unsexy to stop and ask if your partner is

comfortable continuing, but rape and sexual assault

are not sexy either. When you start dating talk about

sex with your partner, before you get down and

dirty. It may be awkward but better to have the

conversation and avoid that awkwardness when you

are both naked. You need to know beforehand

where each other's boundaries are so no one feels

pressured in the moment to try something they are

not comfortable with. And I know it doesn't happen

that way a lot. My first few sexual relations did not

involve the conversations before hand. Sex just

happened. But after what I went through that

Halloween party morning, that talk is now the

sexiest thing I can think of. If you don't have the talk before hand, then make sure you ask when you start to get undressed and before you try new things. Don't start having sex and randomly stick fingers or other body parts in new locations before asking, "is it ok if I try this?" And do not get pissy if they say no. Not everyone is into everything. If you can't deal with that possibility then do not have sex until you can.

Another thing to realize is that just because someone has kissed you, had sexual contact with you, or had sex with you, does not mean they will or have to ever again. You do not have the right to someone because you had an experience with them once, twice, or even for the last twenty years. Even if you are married to them, their body still belongs only to them. That is why talking is such a good idea. If you are going to have multiple encounters with a person, sit down with them and talk about possibilities and boundaries. There are some people, that will let you sleep with them while they are asleep. There are. There are some who want to be woken up with morning oral. Who want to try new things without a conversation first. And that is ok, and normal, but you cannot know if you are with this type of person if you do not ask first. And even after you have had this conversation, even after you know it is ok to do this or that, the other person still retains their right to tell you no at any point. If every single night he or she has let you have sex without a condom or with a finger in their butt, and they tell you no on this particular night, you do not have the right to be angry or force the matter, or put pressure on them to change their mind. You cannot say, *"well you always have before, you can't change the game after ten years."*

Yes, they can. We always have the right to say no. To change our minds. To suddenly dislike something we have always enjoyed. We do not lose our right to our body or our personal desires at any point in any relationship. But people do not acknowledge this.

The guy who touched me that morning, sexually assaulted me. But the world disagreed with this. Because I had slept with him previously. Because I let him sleep over in my bed. I am going to tell you something very personal. The night before this experience, he had come over, we had started to kiss and have sex, like every other time.

Then he asked me, if I had ever tried anal and if I

wanted to. I had never been interested in it, but in

that moment after two months of him being fun and

respectful, I decided, why not? I told him ok, I

would try it, but I wasn't sure I would like it so if I

wanted to stop we had to stop immediately. He

agreed, we tried it, and then after wards we fell

asleep. That is the way new sexual experiences

should go. You want to try something you ask, they

say yes, you try and keep in mind that they may be

uncomfortable and want to stop and you accept that.

But the next morning, the same guy who had asked

before every other new experience, decided that me

being asleep, unconscious, and not capable of

having that conversation, was no longer a deterrent

for his sexual needs. That is when it became sexual assault. That is when I felt betrayed, violated, used, and terrified of what could happen next. That is how easily sex can become nonconsensual and terrifying. That is why we need to talk about this.

I went online at one point after this happened searching for why he would think it was ok to have sex with my body while I was asleep. And let me just say, if you ask your partner before hand, is it ok if I have sex with you while you are asleep and they say of course, or sure unless I tell you not to one night, or yes in this situation, then that is consent. As long as you respect the parameters they set forth and respect their right to change their mind, then it is consensual. But that is not the case of the situations I found when I went online. I found the most horrifying truth imaginable.

There is this website called topix.com. It is a forum where you post questions. Someone posted this, *"Did you ever finger your wife/girlfriend while she was sleeping?"* There were over two hundred responses.

"I do it almost every night to my girlfriend wit out her even knowing it!!! I can slowly get 3fingers in her with out waking her!"

"I let a friend of mine finger my wife when she went to bed after drinking a bit too much. She woke up really horny the next morning and we had great sex. Now I'm waiting for the right time to let him f# ck her while she's sleeping. I'd like

her to wake up with his hot load dripping out of her!"

"I finger my wife while she sleeps.. she gets really wet then I stick it in with out her waking up! almost better than if she was awake ..last time I did this I came fast!!"

"I've also managed to finger her anally also had to fingers in to the hilt she never woke up because of the meds I guess. She would never let me do that while shes awake. Last time i had her going good slipped her panties off and about to Stick it in for real then she kinda started to wake so I left her like that without her panties on till morning. Its was so hot."

"I finger my wife all the time while she is sleeping. She resists so I have to be very careful.

Sometimes she actually snores while my fingers

are insider her, so she is either great pretender or

sound asleep. I love it, it turns me on and most of

the time she is really horny the next day. Which is

not normal. Sometimes I insert my fingers withe

her clothes on . The other night I had three fingers

inside her right through her pajamas. She was

getting really wet when she woke up and rolled

over."

Reread those. Read them again.

"She resists so I have to be careful."

"I let a friend of mine finger my wife when

she went to bed after drinking too much."

"I've also managed to finger her anally also

had to fingers in to the hilt she never woke up

because of the meds I guess. She would never let me do that while she's awake."

"This is something I do every night. I usually cannot do to sleep unless I slide my kok into my girl's sleeping p*ss. She's a heavy sleeper and doesn't wale up at all. It's the best when we go out for some drinks and I know I can position her anyway I want. The best is when I pull her on top of me and thrust up into her and she doesn't wake up. That makes me cum hard!!

As a matter of fact, I just slid into and came about 45 mins ago. I get her into the spoon position most nights and go to town."

Two hundred comments like those. Do you know how I feel when I read those? I feel like crying. I feel like tracking down the girlfriends and wives of these monsters and telling them to run. I feel like never letting a guy touch me again. These are the answers you see all over the web when you look up, *"sex while I am asleep."* It took until page seven out of thirteen on this website to have more than one, *"Guys this is not ok,"* comment. And those are laughed at, ignored. She gets wet so obviously she likes it. She probably just pretending to be asleep.

On a website called,

marriedpeopleproblems.com there is an article or comment about having sex with your sleeping wife. The article approaches it reasonably suggesting why it may be something men think is ok and why women don't always agree and how to maybe talk about it, but in the comment section, I found this,

"It could be worse, he could be with another woman. Women who are married or in a serious relationship should not feel used or abused ,he must love your body to have sex with you whether you are alert or TKO'd. Embrace your man ,because he loves you enough to not go ASTRAY. And never deny him of SEX , F**k him til his rod hurts & he screams no more please. AND NEVER TRY TO PUT HIM ON PUSSY CONTROL AGAIN...."

Almost every comment on that page echoed this comment. Let me break down what these men are saying.

If you are married, your body no longer belongs to you.

If your man is fucking you while you are asleep, be grateful he isn't cheating on you because obviously he isn't getting it enough when you are awake.

If you are married or in a serious relationship, because obviously he loves your body enough to have sex with it, you should not feel abused.

I want to make something abundantly clear to every single person in the entire world:

If you perform any sexual act whatsoever on another person without their explicit consent... It is RAPE. SEXUAL ASSAULT. and AN ACT OF SEXUAL VIOLENCE.

If you at any point have done something sexual to someone without their permission...
YOU ARE A SEXUAL ASSAULTER. A RAPIST.

If someone has performed a sexual act on you without your permission, through coercion or threats, through the use of drugs or alcohol, through using their authority over you to pressure you.. YOU ARE A VICTIM AND A SURVIVOR OF A SEXUAL ASSAUIT OR RAPE.

There may be grey areas here. What if both of you are drunk or high? Is kissing the same as touching or is touching one part of the body perceived differently then another? But that is why we need to talk about this. And I know that all this can happen to men too and I am in no way trying to

218

minimize that. I think we need to talk about the male perspective too, but I am a girl. I am seeing these conversations from the girl's persecutive. I am looking at the statistics involved and I am looking at the way the world acts towards my female self. I cannot put myself in the male perspective without it feeling fake and in-genuine. So I am going to let a guy talk about the male perspective, and I am going to focus on the female.

As a female, as a girl, when I read those comments, and when I remember every time I walk down a street being 'complimented,' and then look at the statistics, and then hear about 'rape culture,' one message starts to come across very clearly; **I am not allowed to enjoy sex without being a slut, but my body is there to be sexed and enjoyed by**

men whether I want it to be or not. I belong to men, to be looked at, spoken about, touched, and penetrated. It doesn't matter if they care about me and I trust them, my body is theirs and it is my fault that they need sex when I am asleep because I am not putting out. I was wearing the wrong clothes and was in the wrong location, so it is my fault. I got drunk. I let him sleep next to me. I let him try anal. So what did I expect?. And really girls when we look at the world we grew up in, is it any wonder that we still go through these experiences?

Let's take a different look at the world I grew up in. Let's take a look at the things we don't talk about and why those might also be important to changing the way I am treated in reference to sex and sexual relationships.

...The Things We Don't Speak Of...

We don't want to talk about the slave trade and child brides. Some of us try, but it's happening over there so why is it our problem?

We don't want to talk about the millions of women who are raped in war time because soldiers need their sexual release. But that doesn't happen here right? We get it, its bad, but it's not here.

We don't want to talk about the girls, who while awake, have their clitorises removed violently with pain and blood, because women shouldn't feel sexual pleasure. After all, in those cultures women are there to bear children. We cringe when we hear about this, maybe we sign a petition, but then we don't try to talk about it any more. Because it hurts to think about.

 We don't want to talk about the women in our military who are raped by their commanding officers. We don't want to talk about the woman raped by police or any other authority figures. They were threatened by the thought of being put in more danger if they did not comply, but it isn't like they were forced right? It was not violent, so it couldn't have been that bad.

 We don't want to talk about the girls who are expected to pledge their purity to their fathers because if they don't, then they have failed their parents. Because that girl's vagina belongs not to her, but to her family and future husband and for her to let someone touch it before then is a crime against that family, that husband, and God.

We don't want to talk about the new studies coming out talking about how women in teaching hospitals under anesthesia sometimes have pelvic exams done to them without their knowledge or consent by students. If you think I am kidding, google it. abcnews.go.com has an article about how ninety percent of medical students have performed pelvic exams without knowing whether the unconscious patients consented or not. Pelvic exams include putting instruments up inside a women vagina. That is happening without the women ever being able to say yes or no. Imagine waking up from a surgery and realizing something feels off down there. And there is no law against this.

We don't want to talk about the fact that girls like sex as much as men. Some like it even more. That we are the ones who could get pregnant but are made incapable of affording or accessing birth control that treats not just pregnancy but many serious medical conditions that are ignored, because birth control means we are being slutty and you don't want to pay for our inability to keep our legs closed.

We don't want to talk about the girls who got pregnant because of the birth control problem but cannot survive a pregnancy mentally, physically, or just simply do not want to be pregnant. Because obviously the very fact that we are capable of getting pregnant should mean that we either want babies or not have sex until we want the babies.

Hormones and sexual tensions be damned. The fetus is more important.

We don't want to talk about the rape culture that exists in our own back yard. On college campuses and by our sports players. They are the town heroes. We need them to go to the championships. So they videotaped themselves raping her while she was so drunk she could barely stand? She drank. It was her fault.

And we don't want to talk about the girls like me. Who had the audacity to trust someone enough to let them sleep in bed next to me. Who had the audacity to believe that when I am asleep, my body is mine. Who had the audacity to be asleep in the moment when he woke up horny and not immediately wake up ready to serve him with my body. Because his needs are the only ones that matter. I may be the one who's vagina can tear and bleed when I am not ready to have sex. I may be the one who can get vaginismus because of trauma and become incapable of sex without pain. But no. I was born with breasts and a vagina, so my body does not belong to me. It belongs to you and your eyes, your needs, and your gender.

We just don't want to talk about sex. At least not in the way we speak about learning to cook, or drive, or get a job. We think that if we teach preteens the basics about our changing bodies and hormones, then everything else they will figure out on their own. Maybe you tell them not to do it, maybe you tell them about condoms and pills. But most of the time you talk about love. How when you love someone sex happens. How you should have sex only when you are in love. We speak about the dangers of disease and babies. But we do not talk about sex. About the realities of sexual relationships. About the grey areas of consent that we all face at some point. We say that yes means yes but we never expand on that. We never talk about how the absence of a no doesn't mean it is a yes. We don't talk about how to talk about sex.

I am not an expert. I will never claim to be an expert. I do not know everything about the different cultures around the world, or about the different religions. I know only what I have been exposed to through history text books, the media, the internet, and my own experiences. Which is why this is not a manual. This is not a how to have sex book. It is not a detailed manuscript on the dos or do nots in your personal bedroom or wherever you choose to do the naked tango. This is simply a book about me and my experiences and the reasons I think we need to start talking.

...The Beauty of Human Sexuality...

Somewhere in the midst of speaking about sex, consent, sexual education, and gender, we must also admit to ourselves that no matter how complex the rules of sex are, human sexuality is just beautiful. Every single human being has some type of inner sexuality. If you are asexual, gay, pansexual, whatever you are, that is a sexuality. How incredible is that? Some people have fetishes in bondage, in bodily fluids, or in roleplaying every possible scenario out there. Sure, some sexual tendencies are looked down upon in society, but the very fact that there are so many different types of sexual interests, and the fact that most of us can ever find even one person who shares our interest with us, how can you not find that so perfectly amazing? How can you not want to talk about it?

The moment my hormones hit, my sexuality was ignited. I would watch anime and read the fan fiction smut just because it was there. My daydreams were always sexual in nature. For me, my sexuality became a huge part of my identity. I don't feel like myself in situations where I know sex is a taboo subject. I strongly feel that cultures and religions that ignore sexuality or try to repress it, should be reexamined and reconsidered. From the feminine perspective, it does seem that most religions are just ways of controlling women. Looking at politics in most places, this theme seems to be continued. Women always get the short end of the stick, which is funny in a sad depressing way because as much as men may not want to admit it, they all came out of vaginas. The world just wants to act like human sexuality doesn't really exist. God and most religions say sex is only for babies, married people, and straight people. Cultures raise us to believe that sex before marriage is shameful and dirty. If you are a female, they try to do everything possible to reinforce within you that sexuality is taboo despite it being used to sell every product in existence. Governments are the male lead testosterone driven forces that write and enforce rules based on these religious and cultural beliefs without once asking what is being sacrificed in the process.

Human sexuality is being sacrificed. It is repressed, hidden, spoken of in hushed voices behind closed doors. We see it in small bursts on ads, in television, and with our partners, but that isn't enough. Human sexuality is unique. It is complex. It is beautiful. We are creatures designed to want sex even when we have no way of knowing if it would lead to procreation. Other animal species only mate by season, or when the female goes into heat. But humans, we have sex everyday. We don't care if it's the right season, or the female is ovulating. We see someone, we get tingly feelings, and then we end up naked and sweaty sexing each other into the night. Because we are designed to want that. Penises and vaginas were designed to feel pleasure no matter what day or season it is. Sex feels good. It feels amazing. We have developed toys, websites, and even special furniture just to increase our ability to have fun in bed. And as much as sex is physical, it is also incredibly emotional.

People cry after sex. We release hormones during it that make you happy for hours if not days after you have it. We get attached to our partners. Some people don't. Some more than others, but there is some type of emotion in sex. Anger, hatred, love, fear, grief, and happiness. We have sex because of every possible emotion. Because that is the beauty of human sexuality. It is flexible and complex. We can use sex to comfort someone, to feel closer to them, to relieve stress, to relieve intense anger, or even just because we were bored. I can barely even find the words to describe what human sexuality is because of how individual it is. Each person has such a different relationship with their sexuality.

Instead of accepting and acknowledging how incredibly complex, individual, and beautiful human sexuality is, we send mixed messages. We use it to advertise, but won't teach kids and teenagers that it is normal. We say wait till you are married, but never tell you what to expect on that wedding night. So when we have problems around sex, when we get confused or afraid or have physical problems that affect our sex, we hide it away. We keep it to ourselves. So it is hard to get help, it is hard to know when you even need to get help or where to go when you are finally ready to leave the shadows. And even worse, even in matters of problems surrounding sex, men are more exposed to information. You hear about erectile dysfunction all the time. I was twenty-two when I first heard of vaginismus, a painful seizing of the vagina that makes it painful to have sex and can be caused by trauma, fear, and STDs. I wrote this book to discuss some of the ugliness surrounding sex. I needed to confront my own trauma and express my dissatisfaction in how the world prepares us for sex. But at the end of the day, part of accepting that there is a dark side to sex, is admitting how beautiful sexuality can be when everything goes right. And maybe the way to start fixing the problems we do have surrounding our sexuality, is to start talking about it in a better light.

...My Name Is...

My name is Olivia Broustra. I am a twenty-three year old law student with an obsession for wolves and a desire to work for wolf conservation. I have been having sex for three years. I was raised in a mostly liberal household by parents who were raised conservative and religious with a younger brother I do not always get along with. I was raised to have a healthy outlook about my body, my mind, and my eventual sexual health. I was taught about masturbation, and told that it was ok to kiss someone I was not in love with. I was told that sex is healthy and normal, but to be careful so I would be safe. I was given access to birth control and condoms and my parents support in potentially terrifying situations like pregnancy. My parents supported me when I made decisions concerning piercings, tattoos, and when I decided to start taking pole dance classes as a way to exercise and explore an empowering and beautiful dance. They even replaced my pole this Christmas when my first broke down. I honestly think every girl should try pole dancing at least once by the way. It is fun, works every single muscle, helps with coordination and flexibility, and is extremely empowering and sexy.

I have been sexually harassed on the streets of every city I have walked through and heard from other girls the stories of their attempts to walk alone, internet date, and just be a female in this world.

I have had relationships and one night stands. I get tested for STDs, and got an IUD because I wanted the extra security. I watch porn and have a box next to my bed with various toys. I am not what you would consider repressed or uneducated by any standard. But that is not all I am anymore...

My name is Olivia and I am one of the one in six American women who has been the victim of an attempted or completed rape or sexual assault. I am one of the two-hundred and ninety-three thousand sexual assault victims of twenty-fifteen. And those numbers only reflect the assaults we know about. Many, many more go unreported. One of the four out of five victims of an assault is committed by a non stranger. I was the victim of a nonviolent sexual assault. Where just my fear of the possibility of what could come next was enough to stop me cold and prevent me from trying to resist or confront the man behind me.

I have been told that it was my fault. That I should have known better. That I should have said no the moment I woke up and realized what was happening.

I live every day with the new reality that every man I sleep next to might touch me without my permission and without me ever knowing it. And while I have managed not to let that make me fear relationships, I have not managed to return completely to my normal sense of myself. My trauma manifests in other ways. In anxiety attacks in class or when I try to read emails from professors. In a constant fear that I will break down and quit school, or hurt myself, or suddenly stop wanting to be with men. It is harder for me to pole dance everyday and there are times when during a dance, even when I am alone, I suddenly feel weird about feeling sexy.

I face every new conversation with a desperate want to scream that this happened to me, so that more people are forced to accept that this is a reality. That it can and has happened to someone you know. You are speaking to someone who survived. I hide it well don't I? Most of us do. When I do tell other women about what occurred a surprising amount will tell me that they too went through something similar. We talk easily about it with each other, but when we speak about telling men it becomes clear, men seem to brush it off. They make excuses for other men. Try to tell us it was a misunderstanding. And other women sometimes say the same. Look at the world we live in they say. We are women. We have to be more careful. Because that is the conversation we have always had. It is our responsibility not to get raped. It isn't his responsibility not to rape.

I got lucky. I guess. My parents and close friends and school have been amazingly supportive and understanding. But I still had therapists and the rest of the world minimize what happened. I wasn't beaten up. He did not force me down and push it in. He did stop before his penis was inside me. So really, how bad could it have been? As if that makes it all better. As if that makes it any less of a violation.

I woke up to another person's fingers inside my vagina. I woke up to him about to push his penis inside of me with no care or concern for whether I wanted to have him inside me that morning. He even admitted to me later that he would have continued if I had not woken up. Even when I did say no and push him away he did not immediately stop. He tried again. Told me he knew I was ready. Because obviously he could read my mind and my no was just, I don't know, not important. All it took was one morning, one guy's horniness, one man's disregard for whether I was present or not in my own body, and suddenly my world is completely different. I had always known that as a girl I was at a high risk for this to happen. I hear the way guys call out to me on the street. I see the way they look down my shirt or at my ass. I hear and read the things guys say to each other about girls online, on tv, and on the street. I was not naive to my reality as a girl. I don't get in strange men's cars, I always meet in public the first few dates, I have a taser, I don't walk alone in certain places. I don't drink from strange bottles or leave my drink unattended. But none of that mattered because my attacker, was the person I trusted enough to sleep with weekly. He was the one who did everything right for two months. Who asked permission before everything else.

So we need to change the conversations. We need to stop pretending that anyone except for the attacker, the rapist is responsible. We need to stop acting like if you follow all the rules nothing will happen to you. You can be sexually assaulted and raped by your best friend, your boyfriend, your husband, the police, your military commander, the nice guy in the bar, the creep in the parking lot. I hate to say it, but I now live in a world where every single guy I see is a potential rapist. I don't let that stop me from trying to have relationships, but I also can't stop myself from thinking that. And again I know girls can be rapists too I really do. But that is for someone else to write about. Me, I needed to write about my girlhood, and his manhood. Because that was my experience.

So we need to change the conversations. We need to talk about consent. About boundaries. About respect. We need to tell boys that despite what they hear or see around them, girls are not there just to be sexual objects. Girls do not owe guys anything. Our clothes, our mannerisms, our jobs mean absolutely nothing about what we may or may not be willing to do in bed or with you. And we need to tell boys that that is ok. That girls can say no. That girls can walk the streets without you having to acknowledge them. We need to tell girls to stand up for ourselves. We need to know how ok it is to say no and if we do, and that boy gets angry, that is not ok. The fear you feel does not mean you are weak, it means that you are no longer in a safe and comfortable situation and that is not your fault. It is only the fault of the person making you uncomfortable. Using force or threat or coercion or your mental state against you. We need to teach the difference between a yes and the absence of a no.

But more than this, we need to teach men about the world we as women live in. We need to explain to them why just fear is enough to stop us cold. Why we never want to walk alone. Why those compliments are not compliments. We need to teach boys from a young age that the way the world looks to us is so different and so scary compared to their own, that we never know how to say no. Because we are always afraid of what happens next. I was. That girl in the bar shifting uncomfortably trying to sidestep the conversation with the over eager guy, she might be so scared of him that she doesn't know how to walk away. The sad fact is, in order for us women to eventually live in a world where we are not just statistics waiting to happen, cum dumpsters, living fleshlights, or possessions, we need to change the way men are taught to look at us. Because the sad fact is, for the moment at least, this world is predominantly run by men. They are in power and are the ones making the laws that we have to follow. They do not go through periods, or pregnancy scares, or abortions, or street harassments. They do not go through life being reminded that they have breasts, that their pussies should be pounded like the sluts they are. They do not look around at the rest of the world only to be reminded that their self worth is reliant on the fact that they have perky breasts and a tight little hole. But remember if to many men have been in that hole, that's just disgusting. They are the ones making decisions about our access to birth control and abortions. The ones responsible for giving us justice when we speak out against our attacker.

We need to remind the fathers, brothers, husbands, boyfriends and male best friends that the girls they love are being constantly subjected to the realities I have described. Because for the moment, they are the ones who can help fix it. They are the ones whose voices can be heard the loudest. Which brings me to another point.

We need to start listening to the girls. We need to start respecting what women say. Teaching them from a younger age that their voices matter too. That even though we may not be heard as much as the boys, we should never stop trying. We should keep yelling and screaming until the world starts to listen. Starts to hear us. Because our experiences matter too. And until they matter as much, until our voices are considered as important as those of our male counterparts, we cannot stop screaming. Because this is the year twenty-sixteen. Our world is changing quickly. We finally have laws allowing two men and two women to marry. Transgender individuals have more and more role models out there. We have instant access to information and can finally see the horrors and the miracles of this world in a moment's notice. We elected a black man president twice, and now have a woman running and doing well in the next presidential campaign. We have movies about BDSM and male strippers. Tv shows like Jessica Jones finally tackling the darker issues like rape and exploring the world of feminism. So is it not about time for me to walk down the street without fear of being attacked just because I dared to be born a girl? Is it not time to teach boys and girls how to respect each others' bodies so that just because I am in a sexual relationship, he doesn't think that means he has instant rights to my body? Is it not time to accept that men and women deserve to feel equal in all aspects of life even sex?

...

My name is Olivia Broustra and I am a survivor of a sexual assault. I am a survivor of a world that is constantly telling me I deserve less. I don't deserve to be a sexual being in the same right as the men around me. I don't deserve the same right to safety. The same right to my own body.

But there are girls out there in worse situations. Girls whose sexual organs are removed at the age of puberty while they are wide awake. Girls who are sold every day to new horrific situations that they will not escape from until they are dead. Girls who are forced to marry and have sex when they are still children, before puberty even hits. And there is only one real way to start to fix this. We need to start talking. We need to start screaming until the other half of the world pays attention. We need to force the world to listen, pay attention, and work on new solutions because we cannot celebrate the advancements we have made for human rights without also acknowledging that half of the world, the female half, is still treated like lesser beings, still treated like we belong to Adam because Eve was supposedly made from his rib.

Finally, we need to recognize how beautiful sexuality is. We need to accept that it is a part of our lives and sex is not going anywhere. Teaching people the beauty of sex, could help us fight the negativity that leads to the sexual problems this work has described. So let's start a conversation about every part of human sexuality. Let us bring sex out of the shadows and admit that it is a pretty significant part of life when hormones kick in. Let us stop ignoring the facets of sex that we don't want to see and help those affected by being forced to hide. Let's help sexual abuse victims feel safe admitting that sex became a part of their lives earlier and in a different way than it should have. I am done waiting for the world to accept that I was assaulted. And I am done hiding how incredible I think human sexuality is. I love sex.I love nakedness. I love myself despite every flaw.

I am a survivor. A victim. A daughter. A sister. A lover. A fighter. A tattooed, pierced, pole dancing pixie.

I have depression. Anxiety. and PTSD.

I have been loved. I have been assaulted.

I am a woman living in a predominantly patriarchal world.

I can see how amazing human sexuality is, and how dangerous.

So, this is my scream. My attempt at getting the

world to listen. My truth. My reality. My

experience.

There is really only one thing left for me to say;

I want to to talk about sex, human sexuality, gender,

and our inability to talk about these things, and for

the sake of us all, you should want to too.

So let us discuss the yeses, the noes, and the maybes

we hear during sex.

Let's start talking about sex.

· · ·

www.ingramcontent.com/pod-product-compliance
Lightning Source LLC
Chambersburg PA
CBHW030426290526
45786CB00001B/152